Teaching Without Grades

by MAX S. MARSHALL

Foreword by DELMER M. GOODE

Corvallis:

OREGON STATE UNIVERSITY PRESS

PROLOGUE: *The Love of Learning*

What chance has "the love of learning" in undergraduate life? A courageous freshman wrote the following essay as a theme for a class in English composition.

It is a familiar academic axiom that we must learn for the love of learning, that grades are unimportant, that the student who thinks of grades or works for grades is somehow contemptible, and that learning for the love of learning is the only respectable academic criterion. But anyone who is fool enough to swallow such tripe has not realistically examined the academic situation.

Upon what basis, for example, does one pass a course? On the basis of his love of learning? Hardly! Rarely is love of learning considered by either instructor or student. The instructor is concerned with giving his students competitive grades and with making his course so tough it cannot be called a mickey. Students are concerned with trying to pass the course with better than average grades. They know it does not pay to be average. Men may be created equal, but no one wants to be equal. We all need to be excellent.

It pays to be excellent. Society itself puts a premium upon excellent grades. Newspapers print honor rolls naming those who have made the highest grades. Scholarships at all academic levels are awarded on the basis of the superior grade-point average. Similarly, one goes on probation or is suspended from college, not because he failed to love learning but because his cumulative grade-point average failed to make a two-point. No one bothers to find out who loves learning.

In the business world, an employer going over an application becomes interested in the applicant whose college transcripts show top grades in the necessary subjects and skills. Employers do not ask whether or not the applicant loves learning. Purely social organizations such as sororities and fraternities use grades as a basis for admission to membership, and for initiating or dismissing pledges. Even such things as beauty contests, selection of kings and queens for campus dances, and tryouts for the rally squad are handcuffed to the grade-point average.

In the academic shuffle, grades become all important, and love of learning becomes a fantasy. Who has time to pursue his love of learning? The academic term speeds nonstop from registration to final grade curve. Courses are filled with assignments, tests, term papers, bibliographies, and the necessity for parroting the textbook at appropriate times. The individual student has little leisure to explore the fascinating byways beckoning him off the main course. His four years are overloaded with requirements for graduation, with credits for majors and credits for minors, and with prerequisites for subsequent courses. The cumulative grade-point average cracks the whip.

Only a fool will kid himself that grades are not important and that it is his privilege in college to satisfy his intellectual curiosity. In the world of reality, the love of learning hasn't a chance.

NANCY LEE WALLACE

When a professor of microbiology in another university had an opportunity to read Nancy's freshman theme, he wrote her a letter:

Dear Nancy:

Your "Love of Learning" delightfully mixes brutal frankness and realism. I often tell my students that they have to get their educations in spite of, not because of, the system. They know this so well that they do not even smile as they nod their heads. The reason that we are not even more badly off than we are is that you and your fellow students have your ways to make and cannot afford to let the system beat you. This has been true under other systems, and is one reason why so much debate about different schemata has occurred.

In your fully justified scorn of the existing system, I hope only that you will not forget that the love of learning is the paramount issue for you personally—after you have met society's stupid demands. Grades, as you point out, are a means to reach a goal. Society should learn that what it wants is integrity, talent, a will to serve, and as much love of learning and training as may be possible. To think that grades and degrees measure these things, as you imply, is ridiculous. The illusion which you describe so well is an evasion of responsibility, a preference for the public opinion poll which dodges the need to choose between right and wrong.

MAX S. MARSHALL

REPRINTED from *Improving College and University Teaching,* Vol. 15, No. 1, (Winter 1967), p. 20.

Dr. Max Marshall attracted new attention in the academic world with the appearance in 1951 of his book *Two Sides to a Teacher's Desk.* Here was a microbiologist, a member of the faculty of one of the world's renowned universities, evidencing a keen interest in and perceptive grasp of college and university teaching and its advancement.

Dr. Marshall has contributed more than 100 titles or research papers in microbiology, including several published guide books. Since 1951 he has added a biography, *Crusader Undaunted* (1958) and, as this book goes to press, close to 100 articles on college and university curriculum and teaching.

Teaching Without Grades is a unique book by an author extraordinarily equipped to write it. He has had long actual experience in university teaching without grades. With gracious urbanity yet unequivocal forcefulness he deals with the issues, appreciative of the position of those who believe in and are wedded to the use of grades and at the same time sharply concerned about the destruction of educational values which grades involve. He regards the greatest obstacle against the discontinuance of grading to be the difficulty in grasping a philosophy of nongrading.

He describes a maturely determined procedure for teaching without grades that "has been tried on medical, dental, dental hygiene, pharmacy, nursing, undergraduate and graduate students and closely followed through internships, dismissals, recommendations, scholarships, honors, and careers for over thirty years."

Readers may or may not experience a change in their philosophy, but they may be assured of enjoyment in reading a deeply thoughtful and thought-provoking book. It brings a sober challenge to all of us who teach in college or university.

DELMER M. GOODE

CONTENTS

xi

Teaching Without Grades

1. Putting the Case

AT THE AGE OF FIVE we were supposed to work for gold stars in Sunday School. They were bestowed each week upon the pupils who produced the best coloring of a sketch of some religious theme. I never got a star. In grammar school I recall only one grade, a G in penmanship. This was notably lower than E for excellent. I learned to write legibly as a sophomore in college. I recall not a single grade acquired in high school.

Only two grades in college come to mind. One was a C, my lowest grade that lucky year. It was in physical chemistry, the only subject I understood that term. The other was a 67 in calculus. This was in 1917 when war was in the air and Wilson was sending notes back and forth across the Atlantic. Two years later, when I took the course again, I was awarded a 95. This sticks in my mind because the registrar insisted on leaving the original grade on my record; he would rather fight than switch.

In the graduate school I can recall two events linked with grades. One was in a course in electrochemistry in which the professor let us grade ourselves. Nobody suffered in grades but our consciences were mauled a bit. The other grade was in a course in the theory of light. There were two of us in the class; the other one was a teacher of physics. That time it was the teacher who suffered. He struggled through with the course, finally resorted to teaching us the elements of physics, passed us, and never gave the course again.

Eventually, crossing the line to become a teacher myself, I handed out grades instead of receiving them. The department had a system in which thirty-five grades were recorded for each student in a single course of eight units. At the end of the course it took a week to make the necessary calculations, with errors cropping up right and left. The staff then met and tried to decide where to put the breaks which separated A from B, B from C, and so on. This led invariably to arguments about individual students near the lines of division. Usually an attractive girl would be near a borderline, so the men on the staff naturally lined up against the women. Even then I distrusted myself on grades and gave way to the ladies on the staff. Their biases seemed less misleading but this could have been wrong.

My distrust of grades is not based on an early concern over them. They were credentials one had to get. Except when they were discouraging, my grades were not so high or so low as to make much difference. Teaching, however, introduced troubles with grades. In the graduate school as teaching assistants, we had to read final examinations, or rather we had to grade them—not the same thing. Ten of us lined up in a big room, each reading a question. Someone would call out, "Watch out for Jim here; he's a fraternity brother," or, "Keep an eye on Richardson; the boss told him he'd never pass the course."

Farther along in teaching, with thirty-five grades per student and with most members of the staff avidly curious to see how their friends and favorites would come out, we encountered a student who upset us more than usual. An ex-engineer had transferred to medicine and was now in our class in microbiology. By our arithmetic he finished the course with a potential *D*. A sensible fellow and president of his class, there was no doubt about his eventual graduation. Whether or not we turned in the *D* I do not recall, but he had no later troubles in school and became a physician. The arguments over this man destroyed our faith in our complicated calculations. Quite naively we decided as an experiment to drop all grades and examinations the next year. The experiment lasted thirty years. We had many debates, some of them pitched battles, and we tried many things. Meanwhile, we learned something about some of the angles that pertain to teaching and grades.

This book is not an exhaustive monograph, a review with charts, or the story of an experiment. It is an analysis of the philosophy behind grades, with some of the techniques, pros and cons, and possibilities for a new and better approach. Opponents of grading have yet to win a really significant battle; meanwhile upholders of grades, having been in charge a long time, of course have a side to declare.

The longer one lives without grading, the more he realizes that the principles involved extend beyond classrooms. In a sense, gossip is full of grading and buying a pair of shoes is grading. At times of necessity and sometimes for less excusable reasons, grading creeps into so many facets of our lives that the principles deserve wide and thorough consideration. Debates about grading in schools, almost always based on small issues, need a broader base. With luck, this will appear as we go along.

We may start with an inspection of the sort of information about students that is considered in grading, what information we need and how much, how to get it, and what to do with it when we get it. This might seem to call for no more than a handbook. Before long, however, no matter how much I seek fair play, the goal sought will be put in evidence. The goal is not to discuss how to improve and use a system or the techniques for grading. The aim of this volume is to study ways to avoid scales of purported measurement, declarations of good and bad, or approval and disapproval. If this seems an unlikely aim, it deserves at least a hearing.

2. The Knobby Needs in Grades

CONTROVERSY BEGINS IMMEDIATELY, for we have to make a choice. We may assume that virtually anything that a good teacher can learn about his students will help him to decide how to deal with and how to help each member of his group. On the other hand, we may assume that students are persons with personal rights. If good teachers are responsible only for their subjects, perhaps the fewer things which they know about a student, other than those directly related to assigned work, the better off everyone will be.

To get a reasonable answer in this dilemma we must inspect the main purposes of grading. It will be convenient to divide the several goals for the present into three groups, those seen by students, those seen by teachers, and those seen by administrators.

Other than such significant issues as the need to get good grades to please parents or for other material reasons, students usually assume that grades are based entirely on their work. Grades do serve to bolster pride and they are demanded by society. We are concerned at the moment, however, with the academic function of these marks of alleged merit. Students feel that they want to know how they are getting along during the course, the term, and the year.

This creates a most unscholarly situation, proving at once that the tale of the grade wags the dogged ways of teaching. The simplest way for a teacher to put himself in a position to tell students how they are getting along is to tell them exactly what is wanted and later to reward them accordingly. Indeed, this procedure is often advised. Teachers begin their courses with just such definitions of requirements. Later they base all their examinations on these defined points. At the end of a course a teacher can then reward his students with the precision of a computer. Unfortunately, this system leaves both student and teacher with a nice sense of satisfactory accomplishment. Poor teachers and compliant students can and often do meet on these terms with equal satisfaction but quite perfunctory results. Many a teacher unwittingly wins popularity contests and rides to fame on just this pedagogic technique.

Leslie J. Nason, writing in the *Newark Evening News* (June 8, 1966) said: "When too much dependence is placed upon test grades, teachers tend to teach with the test in mind, hoping that their pupils will make at least an adequate showing."

In a western college a professor wrote to his dean and spread copies of his letter around. He gave the average grade of his students on a national board examination which he had substituted for a final examination. Because his students were ahead of the national average he was quite honestly proud. "We should like to believe that our efforts in teaching may be—in part—responsible for this result." The teaching had been influenced by the planned procedure. Moreover, the flattery of the comparison was inevitable. Students who have just finished a course will naturally produce better guesses on such a test than those who take the test several years after leaving the subject. National boards properly represent the professions for which they stand and citizens at large. They should be especially careful to avoid any influence on schools and teaching. When they collaborate with schools they start a vicious circle based on expediency. Each side seeks accord and mutual praise, blocking the separate methods which put functional right over functional wrong.

To an administrator grading may be part of a bookkeeping system which helps to reduce his troubles. With a good recorder and secretary, he has a means for meeting arguments with or about students. The rulebook and the computer furnish data which can be neatly matched. No administrator can possibly see a student's work in each of his courses, even if he knows all the subjects. By reliance on the teacher's grades, he can apply the rules and sit back securely, whether he is regretting a dismissal or putting on his cap and gown to bestow a medal.

Both administrators and students are forced into high degrees of expediency. The real problem lies on the desk of the teacher, from whom both the student and the administrator get their data. The teacher is the one who is in a position to make direct observations.

How much and what does a teacher need to observe? Some teachers acquire an amazing amount of information about their students, some of it little more than gossip. Teachers with this interest and talent, however, usually make good use of what they know. Little of their information is directed at grades.

It is surely a function of a teacher to help students, combining the talents available, his and the student's. A high school student wants to get into college; a college student plans to do graduate work. Unfortunately, grades are current entrance fees. When a teacher is morally sure that a student with such ambitions can make good, should he help that student along by squeezing a little on grades? Many an honest teacher will say "yes," thereby horrifying the purists

who claim that their arithmetic systems ignore such items as
personalities, ambitions, dress, athletic talent, and future
promise, acknowledged to be important but regarded by
them as improper influences on grades. Consider the ethics
of the member of a board in New York who, when cornered,
informed the press that his group never changed grades;
they simply did not record failures! Is such a policy defiance
of the law, a violation of ethics, or a sign of good teaching?

For abstemious teachers who favor restriction of information to a limited phase of observation, the criterion of
worth or major yardstick is *performance*. These teachers
argue that their task is to teach only their subjects and that
the function of grades is to accumulate a record of satisfactory or unsatisfactory performance. These teachers deliberately wear blinders to prevent influences not, as they
see them, directly pertaining to performance in their courses.

On a memorable occasion a lady on the faculty, polished
in her use of expletives, came at me with eyes shooting
flames. It seems that, officially and in answer to his query,
I had told her chief that such and such a student was on
probation. The chief had mentioned the fact to his staff. In
unmistakable terms the lady claimed that I was deliberately
hanging a special handicap on this fellow's bootstraps. The
information prejudiced all members of the staff, she said,
giving no chance at all to a student who was already under
abnormal stress. My suggestion that knowledge of the student's trouble might also be interpreted as a means for giving him a lift or a little special help fell on deaf ears. I was
a scoundrel of the blackest shade. One learns from such experiences. You may personally want information in order to
help, but your associate may prefer that you keep the information to yourself. Since time to help is never adequate, a
teacher properly has to decide how much the talent and

effort of the student warrant help at the expense of other students.

The question raised by the irate teacher has a little of the flavor of court procedures. Our judicial system uses a highly restricted definition of acceptable evidence. Any point which could possibly be called prejudicial is ruled inadmissible, even though it has been recorded and told to the judge and jury. The lady with the lively tongue sought to exclude evidence which to her introduced an improper bias. Many would agree with her. Asked to define legitimate evidence, in a positive sense, she would have stumbled momentarily, and then would have mentioned examinations, knowledge, and similar items which can be summarized as *performance*.

Those who, with the irate lady, want to limit themselves to acceptance of a ritual in seeking a basis of appraisal will stress performance. They accept this as specific and final. Quizzed, they would cite their personal systems, so much weight given for term papers, so much for midterm examinations, and so on. Although this procedure represents their considered choice, it is not definition; it is no more than a technique. What is performance?

Purists of this sort, anxious to record only observations relative to what they personally call performance in the subject for which they are responsible, when pinned down usually indicate that their efforts refer to some measure of how well their students obey instructions. The teacher sets standards, techniques, and assignments, and the students are expected to follow through. Superficially viewed, this seems reasonable. That is, the teacher has in mind certain procedures which, if performed, are supposed to give the students a grip on the subject. Since students carry out these prescribed acts incompletely and with varying degrees of efficiency, to indicate this degree of completion and competence seems proper.

A second look at this plan raises doubts. The generally acknowledged lack of agreement on allocations of grades verifies the validity of the doubts. The principle of the completed assignment may fit the parent and child, or the employer and employee, but such relationships are not parallel to the complementary accord hopefully sought between teachers and students. Parents have responsibilities for general upbringing in which mental development takes its own pace, and employers have to see that certain work is done. The function of teachers is focused on individual mental development. Though the three functions overlap, the obligations of teachers, parents, and employers are each separately unique.

In microbiology the performance of manipulations in the laboratory is often a moot question. We had an advanced course in which most of those enrolled wanted to become hospital or public health technicians. Our course was required groundwork for another special course, given by another department for such technicians. It was our custom to present techniques in the laboratory as principles, offering our own methods only as our preferences, not as the only ways to perform. Students sometimes found acceptable variations of their own. Our course went on for five years before a war intervened, after which I discovered that we had been putting our students in grave jeopardy. The later course for technicians was designed on the basis of absolutes in performance. By this standard, to have several ways to perform was sinful. Worse yet, the thought that a student might perform in his own way, provided he met the principles, was worse than gross negligence.

Excessive emphasis on the completion of assignments can be absurd; but so can be excesses of emphasis on behavior. One has only to think of a course in English, for example, in which a grade is notably reduced because a student wore an outlandish costume, yet this has happened. The extent to which this problem is within the province of a school is a separate matter of controversy not germane to the present issue. The point is that the costume has nothing to do with the understanding of English. A grade based only on the degree of completion of assigned work is equally, though less clearly, to be classed as a poor measure of understanding of the subject.

The student is sent to school to get an education, not to please the teachers. A simple test of this is possible. At any faculty gathering, look around the room at those you know. No more than a glance will be needed to demonstrate that the task of pleasing everyone there would require that a student be either a hypocrite or an unscrupulous diplomat.

The school's function is to offer students an opportunity to get an education. This would seem to require that teachers think more in terms of the progress of a student toward that end than in terms of narrow inspections of the completions of assignments. Though the defenders of grades contend, with some truth, that each teacher's responsibilities are limited to his or her courses, teachers are not just lone workers in their own corners; they are also members of a faculty which collectively provides the opportunities for the composite known as education. There is no course which provides an education.

To grade only on the assignments in a course, for example, does not measure improvement. The question of whether or not a student who improves notably should be regarded as more worthy than an apt student who coasts at half speed can stir up feverish debates. Further topics of debate will appear as we go along. Suffice it for now to point out that a teacher who wants to know about a probationary status in order to help that student intelligently, so far as possible, seems offhand to be on the right track. The teacher who assumes complete authority and is bent on weighing performance, in the sense of how well pleased the teacher may be, seems to be self-limited, restricting himself to the use of a rigid yardstick in a situation which demands an adjustable one.

3. Exigent Examinations

THE MOST POPULAR WAY to get information about the work of students is to put questions and inspect answers: the examination, quiz, or test. The principle of examination appears deceptively simple. To ask a question and to note how well the question is answered seems offhand so easy a process that misunderstandings would be impossible. The process is complex indeed, however, especially when viewed as a teacher sees it.

"The dog is black," says the teacher. "What color is the dog?" he asks later. "Black," says the student. "Correct," says the teacher. But is *colorless* incorrect? Would you call wrong such answers as *very dark*, or *pink*, based on the skin? Devotees who use examinations as major criteria for grades usually follow the formula of the black dog. This formula is not a teaching procedure; or to be accurate, at its best it can be only a small phase of teaching. Asked for the answer to eight times seven, students can be held to exact replies, but this sort of routine information is no more than a background in teaching arithmetic. Until a man learns what a spanner wrench is he cannot study its uses.

Gauged by purposes, examinations come in three principal types, with a dubious fourth. The first is the simple "black dog" type, an examination for a knowledge of essential basic facts. As a feature of teaching, it is important but secondary. When I was in college, calculus was taught by the wise head of the department. He opened his course in integral calculus belligerently. Pointing to a page of strange formulae, he announced that there would be an examination the next day on all of them. He then added that we needed them as tools, quickly available to us; the understanding would come later. To us this was unusual candor. We thought we knew that in college step one was to find out what we were supposed to know; the next move was to know it and hope for an *A*. This teacher had put his cards on the table and said that papers would not be graded. The next day he said that he would assume from then on that we knew the formulae, and he paid no further attention.

A second type of examination is based on the urge to *test*. Something is supposed to be understood. The teacher wants to test whether or not the idea went over. The point of view introduces an opportunity for unwarranted dogma. The teacher is inclined to use the black-dog type of question, fishing for his chosen answer. If, with a large class, he uses readers, he instructs the readers as to what *he* wants. His goal is the recited answer rather than understanding. Inexperienced readers cannot follow the minds of students through the intricacies in answers to thought-provoking questions, so well-reasoned answers are not separated from guesses and illogical answers.

Whether or not examinations with this purpose in mind are permissible, testing rather than teaching, is debatable. For a teacher to be concerned with how well he has taught, with an interest in how well the students are able to comprehend, is natural. But whether he wonders what students can recite or how well he has taught them to recite, the focus is shifted from the main task at hand, to teach. Of course teachers should seek means for improving their teaching.

Of course they have to know something about the knowledge of their students. These points are axiomatic but secondary. The propriety of using examinations for such purposes is limited. The attitude reaches its peak with deliberately devised "tests," which are in no proper sense examinations.

This type of cold test includes a large category not really involved in teaching. Sometimes found in classrooms, however, this group is worth mention because of the tendency to put all examinations under a common heading. Examinations are frequently used to sort persons into plus or minus groups: personnel tests, Civil Service tests, national board tests in professions, and the like. Their purpose is often nullified by grading them. The purpose of such examinations or tests is only to make a decision, *yes* or *no*. One cannot hire half a man or seventy-six percent of him. Board examinations, designed only as screens to eliminate occasional improperly qualified persons, normally say *yes* to most applicants. Grading plays no part in this process; sorting into two piles is not grading. These are truly "passed" and "not passed" tests.

The third type of examination, functionally grouped, is the kind used as an aid in teaching. Its use is frequently overlooked. Examinations make excellent tools in teaching. If grades can be put aside for the moment, this concept will gain in stature. Grades often dominate and submerge this most valuable purpose.

Examinations used for teaching require the posing of wide open questions, ones which will call forth answers based on total experiences, in and out of the course. To accomplish this there can be no preconceived answers in the teacher's mind. The question is ideal only when there is no absolute reply. Nothing in the text, lecture notes, or other source of answers should fit the situation. Recitation thus barred, thought is then mandatory to produce any response. The teacher has to keep in mind his own true function and

that of his examinations. This is the precise opposite in concept from the viewpoint which obtains under the influence
of grades.

This purpose of examinations, using them to teach, is a
pleasurable challenge in teaching. The use takes a little
practice; no superficial trial will be effective. If he will per-
sist, the teacher can reach a stage of concentrating on good
questions, not even thinking about an answer when he makes
out questions. Answers are up to the students. He hopes that
there is no answer because more is learned by chewing on
good questions than by grinding out routine answers. He
becomes curious to know what different students will do
with it.

He has to realize, too, that students can enjoy this challenge only when they have convincing assurance that they
are really free to answer as they see fit. Otherwise they will
deliberately seek far-fetched answers because they think
that their imaginations are under test, or they will recite from
texts or notes on the assumption that such answers are not
subject to censure. When they learn that they are not graded
in mind, on papers, or in records, and are not measured by
preconceived answers, they will respond and will tackle
severely challenging questions with enthusiasm. An illustra-
tive examination early in the course will help to assure them
that they can proceed with confidence. Teachers have to
practice before they reach the point of ignoring preconceived
answers. With grades, the use of such valuable examinations
as tools becomes so difficult as to be almost impossible.

Stumbling on the teaching examination as a new virtue
of nongrading after some years of teaching without grades,
it occurred to me that I better try my own challenge to see
if I could answer my queries. The questions usually went to
press several weeks in advance. By testing time the questions
themselves were usually forgotten. Taking the examination,

usually at the same time that the students took it, questions often put me in a quandary. The difficulty was aggravated by the fact that as the teacher I had to figure out in advance the several viewpoints that might appear in the assortment of answers. Often I missed opportunities which occurred to the students. The easiest way to catch all points that might arise was to cheat. After reading a few papers I had nearly all the possible answers. This made answering easy for me, but the method was unfair. My answers, good or bad, went on the bulletin board when papers were handed back.

The fourth and dubious type of examination, the test made out of curiosity, is a branch of the second type mentioned. Psychologists, who dislike to admit that man's complexity is beyond tests, continue to build sets of questions on the theory that the right kind of test has not been found. They thus become inordinately devoted to surveys. Under proper control and with due consideration of others, students included, curiosity is a mainstay of education. It can also be one of our most sinful of qualities, constituting an imposition that accepts no boundaries.

A more common way to classify examinations is by form rather than by purpose. The entire set of possible forms that examinations can assume makes an imposing array. To simplify the problems, they are usually first subdivided under two headings, objective types and essay or subjective types. The terms are so familiar that they have become more trite than meaningful. That the terms are inappropriate need not prevent a look at this classification.

Objective examinations are supposed to present perfectly definite questions with definite answers, allowing a computer to be used to read them; or, a microbiologist or secretary could read papers in an examination in vector analysis and come up with the same graded answers as a mathematician. The true/false tests and their assorted imitations are in this category, most of them forms offering multiple choices among given answers, sometimes by frightfully devious mechanisms.

Subjective tests, by this common terminology, include questions which call for the use of words and the creation of answers, rather than marking an x after an answer with a special stylus on purported answers already provided. Usually labeled "essay questions" because they grant students the privilege of saying what they mean for answers, these riddles range from the absurdly general to the notably restrictive. Such a lazy request as "Discuss what you got out of the course" contrasts sharply with the opposite extreme, an open completion type, such as *"Milk may either sour or spoil on standing, because . . ."* The ultimate in the completion type would have to be classed as objective, however, as: *"The whale is regarded as a*............................ *because it produces its young by* ...." In this situation the teacher is after personally chosen answers, the major feature for qualifying as objective. That students manage to answer this type without drawing upon their naturally puckish imaginations to provide ludicrous answers is a tribute to the strength of their self-restraint.

This split of examinations into objective and subjective is appropriately confusing. An example of the multiple choice examination, in one form or another the most popular type called objective, might read:

When was the electric light invented?
1620   1879   1066   1881   1810

Fortune magazine (May, 1966) furnished samples of authentic questions on economics, remarking at the end that anyone who got them all "right" would know more than the teachers. This is one of the easier ones:

Of the following factors, which one is not likely to in-crease the demand for bricks?

> (a) An increase in the price of home construction.
> (b) An increase in the incomes of potential home builders.
> (c) A decrease in the price of mortar.
> (d) An increase in the price of lumber.

If you have trouble in proving that any one of these could be the wanted answer, depending on circumstances, just put the question to anyone who has studied law. In the scientific sense, this sort of test is no more objective than Whitman's poetry.

Teachers usually formulate their own multiple choice questions. They are then inspected by whoever may be coerced into looking at them. Professional testing experts may intrude or are sometimes called in to check over questions or even to originate them. The creator furnishes answers which to his mind are preferred. All those concerned supposedly agree that each choice of the possible answers offered really is the one preferred. All phases of these questions are subjective. Instead of being open, they are restricted to the examiner's mind. The person who reads the questions and seeks an answer is forced to interpret both the questions and the possible answers in exactly the same way that the designer does. Though he may be an engineer taking a course in Shakespeare, he is expected to think as some specialist or psychologist thought.

The multiple choice type of examination puts an expected answer before the student and asks him to guess which it is, neither allowing nor demanding articulate expression or understanding. If he knows his teacher and is good at games, he is moderately safe. He is denied the right to put his answer in the environmental set of ideas on which his choice is based. Examiners expect a single interpretation of the question, although a principal point in law is based on the realization that words are not easily interpreted. Answerers must make guesses as to what is preferred; whereas any carefully constructed question in this form will include at least three reasonable answers which, because each depends on a certain point of view, could be justified in court.

Multiple choice examinations penalize especially two groups who have valuable attributes, experience, and conscientiousness. Experience enlarges the outlook, so that several choices of answers are recognized as reasonable and may hence be the ones sought. Conscientious students search their minds for true answers instead of the ones the inquirer has in mind. Both these commendable groups are more likely to go astray than average students who are geared to answers wanted. Furthermore, the tests put before students whole sets of wrong and confusing answers at a time when their impressionable minds are working at capacity under stress. If the student is in doubt, and these tests make sure that he will be, he will have forced on his attention many more dubious answers than acceptable ones.

No matter how well made, the so-called objective examinations are not a proper part of teaching. As sorting mechanisms, quite possibly they may be of some practical use. In Civil Service or personnel work, for example, in which *yes* or *no* is the only answer needed, the only qualification for a test is a just selection of the highest possible number of genuinely pertinent answers. Unfairness, rather than the evils mentioned with reference to teaching, becomes the paramount issue in multiple choice tests used only for sorting, because the biases of examiners are inevitable in questions.

Consistency in answers is given an undue priority by those of the objective school. They would like to exclude such extraneous factors as the differences in rating answers which occur with deviations in the ways readers' luncheons are setting on their stomachs. Objectivity in the scientific sense puts an excess of faith in consistency. Much of alleged science puts too much faith in a figure or a set of data, fundamentally this same intrinsic error. With a little imaginative effort, we can instruct a class that two and two are really five, whereupon they will add consistently, though in error, until the rules change. As we shall see, escape from responsibility is often a motive which lies in disguise behind an exaggerated approval of objectivity, consistency, and of science itself.

The key to satisfactory examinations for teaching purposes is in learning to have no preconceived answers to questions, to concentrate on good questions and, for the time being, to ignore answers. Once the habit, really an overcome habit, is established, students annoy teachers when, during an examination, they ask "Is this what you want?" The reply comes quickly and automatically: "The answer is not what I want but what you want. Your own idea will be welcome, if you can back it up." If he thinks that his answer will stand up, that is his answer, and it deserves inspection on that basis.

Under enforced regulations for the use of grades the application of good teaching examinations, though more difficult, is still possible. With grades students are both mentally and practically obliged to seek answers which will please their mentors. Surrounded by grades, students become so accustomed to this outlook that teachers who wish to use the examining tool have to make an effort to earn the confidence of students by proving that they do allow the freedom claimed. Unless students know that the instructors will honor an intelligent and independent use of their brains, talents, and experience, and will protect them accordingly, they have no choice; they must seek the answers wanted. To ask students to expose themselves freely to education in an atmosphere of the punitive use of grades, low when students fail to meet given expectations, is neither human nor humane.

But even good causes can backfire. Students on an examination given early in our course once misinterpreted words they had heard about our methods from upperclassmen. They deliberately gave me wildly imaginative answers because they had heard that we paid off on originality. More often, when trust has not yet been earned, students will produce answers from something they recall from text or lecture, assuming that this cannot be called wrong. In this event the teacher is obligated to point out that the student has merely recited, with no evidence of his personal grasp of the subject. If he can add that the text or lecturer cited made too bald a statement or had a different point of reference, so much the better. Neither fantasy nor recitation provide satisfactory answers, rarely any more so than those based on poor reasoning or inadequate basic information.

With open examinations, no preconceived answers, and preferably no possible trite answers, reading examination papers is critical. A vast expenditure of time and energy put into making out questions, with little time spent in reading answers, is an inverted outlook. This should be obvious, but it is not, apparently because testing is so often accepted as more dominant than teaching. Little time need be spent on formulating wide open questions ("Do you really think that bacteria form spores *in response to* adverse conditions?"), but answers to such questions have to be read with care. Once grades are put aside, it is possible to get down to the business of helping, or teaching, measured in terms of understanding and reasoning with, of course, some knowledge.

The problem in reading examination papers is not "What do I think this is worth?" but "What can I do to help this student along?" This outlook is helpful to students and readers alike. The discovery that papers may be read enjoyably is a happy one. Once started, the reader is stirred by curiosity as to what the next paper will reveal. Conversing on paper about the subject at hand is stimulating, for the student's mind has to be followed closely. He becomes the individual that he is. This is exactly the opposite from the outlook under grading wherein the student becomes a number to be given identical treatment with all others. The opportunity to stir the able student to further effort and to encourage the hard-working slowpoke by a word of cheer is a welcome one.

4. The Observation Tower

HAVING INDICATED THAT EXAMINATIONS are major posts of observation, with or without grades, we have to inspect some of the other lookout stations used by teachers as part of their work, involuntarily or deliberately.

Even when considered only as tools in teaching, examinations will lead unwittingly to incidental observations. Joe, who otherwise works smoothly and well, has nervous spells and goes to pieces whenever a test comes along. Jane writes such beautiful English that she gets credit for wisdom that is not there. Good examinations with no preconceived answers push grades into the background, but even when they are used, grades with some teachers drop far enough back so that the student becomes a person instead of a marker on a scale. The remarks of an individual are distinctive. Grades, if they must be assigned, can be influenced by depth in understanding, articulation, knowledge, and reasoning. Less attention can be paid to accuracy in producing preconceived answers and how well pleased the reader may be, but with grades this is difficult.

Observations of students do not all come through such documents as term papers and examinations, however. Observations are made even in lectures, in this case sure to be involuntary. A student in my lectures, now a notably able physician, regularly wore a pained expression which appeared to be such a combination of abject boredom and brazen insolence that I had to avoid looking his way. As time went on I gained a bad impression of him. It turned out that this expression was only the normal pose worn during the many lectures he had to hear. But let new lecturers beware of the front row. The attention of its occupants is pleasantly flattering and its students may be eager and worthy. Lecturers, as a boost to their morale, frequently address a favorite whom they know to be really responsive. But the front row is sure to include several students who stare in bright-eyed awe with obvious enthusiasm while their minds are on the evening party.

Discussions with students, formal ones or those casual conversations after lectures or in hallways, bring about further involuntary observations. By nature a good teacher will divide his primary interests between his subject and his students. To think of students as objects to be appraised during discussions is a heinous offense. Since the teacher who grades is appraising and the student fears to reveal faults, grades, whether in mind or recorded, are sure to interfere with teaching. Many a formal discussion is no more than a command performance by students, held before a teacher with his notebook before him as he obviously records his impression of each move.

One reason many of us prefer to avoid psychologists is because of the persistent feeling that we are bugs under a microscope instead of conversationalists concentrating on a subject. A parallel handicap exists with students and masters who seem ready to pick up and record flaws with little sympathy for students as persons. Claims are sometimes made that teachers of English seldom write because they hesitate to expose themselves to criticism. Mental quirks, the answers of students, and the use of English are all vulnerable, and each is disturbing if listeners or readers are more anxious to pounce on trouble than they are to look for the intended interpretation.

It is unreasonable to *ask* a teacher to concentrate on the subject and sympathize with the student, overlooking with reasoned tolerance a few slips natural to the situation, and thus avoiding the distractions caused by a critical attitude. The only respectable relationship between students and teachers is one grounded upon a natural honest dealing. One way to prevent a person from acting naturally is to tell him to do so. Teachers and students have to be naturally compatible rather than circumspect. The removal of all possible obligations to weigh students, especially the habit-forming grades, helps to open the way to a natural compatibility.

The primary focus of interest in teaching is certainly not the book of records; but it is not the student, either. It is the subject under discussion. That is true whether the subject is a topic of the course itself or whether it is apart from the curriculum, such as an article in the student paper or a coming football game. When both students and the teacher forget themselves and each other and discuss the topic, all is well. That each inevitably picks up something personal from the other is not inconsequential but it is secondary. Though it would be improper to instruct inexperienced teachers to act naturally, we can ask that they try to resist the easy pose of the critic in order to pave the way to as much concentration on the subject as may be possible. A lively interest and a resistance to gossip will do much to eliminate the digressive stress on grades and on other forms of negative criticism.

Discussions between teachers and students occur in halls, office interviews, coffee shops, classrooms, lecture halls, and laboratories. Observations are made unwittingly. Joe is exceptionally avid for information and is under foot all the time. Impressions may arise involuntarily that he is a cocker spaniel in friendliness, that he is an eager scholar, that he is posing, or that he asks more than his share and interferes with time due other students. Jane is unknown to members of the staff and seldom says anything, an observation even though it is a question mark. She may be brilliant or stupid, or more than likely she is just naturally quiet and average in interest, effort, and talent, relative to the subject.

In a similar way, side impressions are gained unwittingly when reading the written efforts of students. Unless the subject is English, what the student is trying to say is more important than such matters as neatness, spelling, or the correct use of words. Though no intentional effort is made to search for what writing reveals, other than specifically what the student is trying to say, writing is an exposure to observation. Interpretation of the meaning intended by the student may require marked concentration, but incidental points are at times conspicuous. Joe, though exceedingly logical, is notably misinformed; Jane, though neat, accurate, and as orderly as anyone could ask, writes in a verbose and often empty style, leaving doubts about her understanding.

Let the record show that all teachers do have a *responsibility* to such matters as neatness, spelling, and the use of clear and acceptable English. Teachers of English who have long been criticized by employers, parents, and other teachers because students who have passed courses in English still fail to use the language well, have become legitimately but unfortunately hypersensitive. Not all teachers of English are able, but that can be said for any subject. It so happens that their subject, unlike any others, is used by everyone during all waking hours seven days a week. Against three or four hours of instruction a week spent with teachers of English in a few short episodes in their lives, students are in a position to practice their bad habits elsewhere over a hundred hours a week indefinitely.

A teacher of chemistry, confronted with an examination or a term paper, has a moral and professional obligation to watch the spelling and English and to do something about gross errors, with an eye to correcting, suggesting, and improving. Every teacher carries a significant share of the responsibility for English. What the teacher does not do is distract, penalize, or criticize the student for his use of English, and above all he cannot permissibly degrade a paper in chemistry for mistakes in English.

A student who thinks of *united* and writes *commited*, or of *committing* and writes *committment*, should be given a chance to learn. Scolding, low grades, deliberate oversight, or griping will serve no purpose. The errors should be corrected without prejudice, as a help. Teachers with good will and the knowledge may add a word about the first letters of suffixes or about accents, thereby teaching the student and earning a little gratitude. Differences in backgrounds and in talents for the use and spellings of words are not part of an understanding of chemistry, but teachers do have responsibilities beyond their subjects, notably so with English. The policy of isolation is not valid in teaching, but articulateness is revealing, if observations are legitimate.

Cheating is another form of distraction likely to divert the teacher from his consideration of the student's understanding of the subject and to stir up disoriented observations. Jacalyn, the daughter of Mr. and Mrs. Ted Dieffenderfer, was going to school in Boulder, Colorado. She was given a lowered grade in a course important to her on the grounds that she was alleged to have helped a fellow student in an examination. She was later exonerated from the charge. The spirit of helpfulness is at least part of good will and learning. No move of Jacalyn's, even as charged, indicated any deficiency in her knowledge or comprehension. The understanding of her subject is supposed to be the basis for grades. The family brought suit but the court declined to take any responsibility, and the school was adamant. Students are at the mercy of college authorities and have no real protection in such matters.

The *San Francisco Chronicle* (Apr. 28, 1966) reported that the University of Arizona passed a ruling that teachers could lower grades or even fail a coed for dressing improperly. This puts the teacher in the legal position of the true despot.

A ruling of the Senate of the University of California (Berkeley), article A1279, visualized the writing on the wall in the expansion of grades to include pontifical judgments along with all scholastic qualifications by declaring that "an academic grade of F may be challenged on grounds that it reflects other than appropriate academic criteria." The rule then goes on to explain the machinations of making such a challenge. The process could be guaranteed to discourage any but the most ardent admirer of red tape. Be it noted, also, that the right of appeal does not go beyond the academic authority itself.

Cheating on examinations shocks many persons. The shudder over cheating is much overworked. Unexcited analysis will prove that each person has his own concepts of what constitutes cheating. A student who copies an article and turns it in as his own is regarded by all as guilty; but just how much paraphrasing converts an article to one the student may call his own is by no means a matter of agreement.

Cheating does not point to a character which is sure to lead to jail. It is usually a response to pressures applied by teachers who ask for excessive details, demanding a mental recall that is difficult for many otherwise able students. It is a consequence of temptations which arise from poor questions, those in which "right" answers are imperative and good answers are called unsatisfactory. Cheating is definitely one of the evils helped by grading as one of its causes. Frantic to produce what the teacher wants, because this unrestricted authority can and will drop a low grade with one stroke of his pen when he is not pleased, it is small wonder that students at times get desperate.

With good questions, even with grades, cheating is virtually impossible. Ask why it (is/is not)a good idea to end a sentence with a preposition and clearly no logically supported answer can be called right or wrong. Omit the fear of a low grade by assurance that no grade will be given or recorded, and the question may even have a personal appeal. For a theme on this question plagiarism would be possible, though it would be unlikely; on an examination, cheating would be almost impossible. Ungraded, he who seeks to answer must take a stand and do some creative work which requires comprehension. In working out an answer, some educational progress occurs.

The theme, notebook, quiz paper, report, and other documents, though noted primarily as expressions of meaning, nevertheless bring observations from the side. Joe is remarkable for his willingness to compile, but the assembling means more to him than the content; Jane is exceptionally thorough. But when grades are used, the attitude of an inspector dominates. Does the document meet my (or the boss's) standards, and how do I like it? In this frame of mind, a neat paper will pick up five or ten unmerited points, one with no margins will lose a few improperly, and a knowledgeable cheater may fail entirely, especially if the teacher happens to think of the writer as an irritating fellow. The removal of grades when observing written evidence helps significantly to permit and even to direct attitudes toward the real purposes involved.

The laboratory, when part of a course, is an excellent place to work directly with students. The task of a teacher in the laboratory is still guidance in the direction of understanding. If the course happens to be vocational, such as practice in the art of lettering, technical aid may well be in order, for the students then seek proficiency in something they hope to use. In courses in biology or chemistry, however, skill is usually secondary. The laboratory is used primarily to provide for direct manipulation and observation in order to gain an understanding. Such understanding is definitely not to be found by reading, listening to lectures, or (despite claims) usually by movies and demonstrations. Understanding, not the "correct" experiment, is the goal. An experiment performed improperly often teaches more than one made in accordance with directions. The cake is not for eating; it is to teach the cook.

In the laboratory a teacher sees each student in action, talks to him as a person, and spends a number of hours with a relatively small group. That a good share of the guidance in laboratories is done by teaching assistants, graduate students with no experience, is in this respect unfortunate. Such aides are good for technical coaching, but from the standpoint of association and opportunities in teaching, experienced teachers miss much by dodging the opportunities in laboratories. True, it is always the students who do the learning. Teachers are persons who deal with learning; there is no such thing as teaching. In the laboratory, learning is an independent process in which a few tips from inexperienced confreres will help the process along. More experienced teachers can probe deeply and pertinently, unless they become bored or impatient. Those who too often take over, gathering students together for chit-chat when students

should have the reins themselves, are suspect. The greater
gains come from helping members of the class when questions are asked, when problems of understanding arise at
the benchside, or during individual pauses.

Observations about students are sometimes based on
hearsay evidence. The fiery lady who objected to knowledge
of a probationary status was objecting to hearsay evidence.
Choosing to be influenced only by what she saw herself, she
regarded hearsay evidence as misleading. The chairman of a
department, on the other hand, may have to be governed in
major degree by hearsay evidence from teaching assistants,
members of his staff, the secretary, and—though this is almost
always inadvertent—even from the students themselves.
Hearsay evidence can be a form of gossip. Discrimination is
necessary. Some teachers make sharp, reasoned, charitable,
and useful observations. Others, unduly influenced by forms
of blindness, curiosity, kindness, defensiveness, mirror-
watching, worship of perfection, and other personal quirks,
are heard with caution.

We return to our starting point. An alert and interested
teacher will make a number of observations which force
themselves upon him. Though it is improper to concentrate
on them, they can be of aid in helping the student along. The
desire to help without hindering in itself brings forth observations. At the end of a term mature staff members may have
to join colleagues from other departments to make decisions
which will critically affect the whole lives of students. For
such students evidence is necessary. The attitude of constant
weighing is gravely reprehensible, however. Most students,
we know, pass their courses and go ahead normally. When
serious troubles or conspicuous talent appear inadvertently
and then only, not before, it is time to take note. To subject
all students in a class to critical scrutiny at every move is
to sterilize teaching.

No two teachers ever see the same set of qualities in a student. Of those that both see, the degree to which each quality is noted is certain to vary. Even when characteristics are seen in about the same degree by two teachers, differences in opinions as to worth are certain. This is not an abnormality which should be corrected by unification, though those who are forever seeking standards so view this situation. It is normal and proper, and as inevitable as breathing.

5. The Information Bureau

In any form, once a collection of information about members of a class comes into existence, something has to be done with it. The route, however indirect, is from the teacher through the front office to the keeper of the records, with all except the last reserving some rights to withhold evidence.

Under grading, the usual procedure begins with ranking the students. Some arithmetic scheme puts them in sequence in order of purported merit. This process is commonly regarded as objective and hence unassailable, because a tradition has it that arithmetic eradicates human factors. An assemblage of symbols, figures in percentages or letters which can be converted into figures ($A = 4$, $B = 3$, and so on), is reduced to a numerical average for each student. That is, figures are weighed and added, say fifty percent for the final examination, twenty-five for a term paper, and the like. The resultant series of figures permits what appears to be an impersonal arrangement of members of a class in an order of alleged competence. Since the figures are juggled with an adding machine, the claim that the result is impersonal protects consciences, but with every factor in this method of calculation subjective and personal, this claim cannot well be honored.

The rank does not always become an official part of the record, but it is used as a means for separating the class into whatever categories are used. For example, though in most pairs there may be a small gap between two adjacent students, near the top there may be a gap of two full points. The upper group then gets *A's* and the lower one gets *B's* down as far as the next gap, which marks the border of the *C's*, and so on. The process, familiar to teachers, seems beautifully simple and reasonably accurate. Figures cannot lie; just people do that. Not all departments regard the lines of division as absolute. The staff, brilliantly observing that the gaps are not great, may consider the names of students near the dividing line to be debatable. Joe is just over the line as a *B* but his laboratory work was abysmal, so, following debate, he gets a *C*. Jane is the other way around. Although she is not very original, she has done good work and is moved up to the *B* group. Besides, she might become a graduate student and need a *B*.

This open exercise of judgment after all the judgments behind the figures have been denied raises the question of what we may call "expedient grading." This principle arouses furious arguments, higher in fever than in wisdom. It is not unreasonable to look upon grades as stipulated symbols which constitute the teacher's recommendations for each student. They are the only votes teachers have in the formulating of final decisions that emerge from deans and recorders, based entirely on observations made by the teachers. Since these symbols are unquestionably used as votes, reason suggests that teachers ought to go the limit to use them to express their advice on future moves.

For example, Joe is on probation. A conscientious fellow but slow, his status worries him and interferes with his work. He will certainly graduate, be an honest workman, and become a solid citizen. Being slow, he is not far up on the

ranking scale. If he is graded a little higher, however, he will
perhaps be taken off probation. In no other way can the
teacher vote to have that probation removed, thereby giving
a little encouragement to a future graduate and improving
his education, by removing from his neck a millstone that is
doing more harm than good. He gets the higher grade, an
expedient grade. Such grading considers the desired effect to
be important, which it certainly is, within reasoned limits
even more important than the student's restricted performance in a course. A department which pulls down its grade
sharply, when a smart but cocky fellow works only at half
speed and uses neither his talents nor his opportunities, cannot ipso facto be accused of either poor observations or poor
teaching.

Members on the other side in this battle consider the
expedient grade to be a heinous offense against the whole
educational system and them in particular. They think of
grades as truly objective, perhaps lacking the precision of
a foot rule but the best that can be devised. To them the
juggling of figures is equivalent to the act of a scientist who
would change the figures of an experiment to suit his convenience.

When these firm critics refer to a teacher who would
give a student a D because of the length of the student's
hair or a girl an A because of her looks, they have a point.
Otherwise, they are victims of an illusion comparable to
such mathematical oddities as the Möbius strip. A figure, say
76.4, is finite and impersonal. It is accurate between 76.35
and 76.449. If the 76.4 represents something, however, instead of being an abstract figure in mathematics, the appearance of accuracy may be purely fictitious. Since every
factor that went into the grade of 76.4 is dubious in a dozen
respects, the potential error in the compiled figure is far
greater than the span of figures in the whole graded class.

To exaggerate the error would be unfair, just as it is improper to exaggerate the significance. These are the figures, however, which are used to establish the relative ranking on which separate categories are based. For a score of years I spent many hours toying with the grades of medical students, examining them relative to other information at hand. I studied both departments and students. The ranking was ridiculous. For critical decisions the most anyone seriously claimed for ranking was that there might be more winners in the top ten than in the bottom ten. Even this was often dubious.

The simple fact is that a small group of ten students can be ranked in precisely 3,628,800 ways. A choice of a single one of these ways seems somewhat precarious. With one more student, 39,916,800 possible arrangements are available, some 36,000,000 more ways than with ten students. A twelfth student would add nearly half a *billion* new possible arrangements. Since our classes were then running about eighty, the selecting of one order out of a number of possibilities that would make the hardiest astronomer blush could not well be called realistic. Any single order looks neatly finite, and no one should be surprised to find that many students land "near the levels expected." Everyone knows that statistics are notoriously tricky, but few, especially when faced with neat figures they want to believe, realize how tricky they can be.

Meanwhile, departments spend hours on grades, recorders pore over their records, committees look at the recorder's figures and suggest to the dean that he send out severe warnings, and students decide that getting better grades is a game that has to be played, rain or shine.

6. And Why Not?

THE PRACTICE OF GRADING is vulnerable and is often challenged. Richard Reynolds wrote a syndicated article which appeared in the *Sunday Oregonian* (Sept. 18, 1966). It is based on a study made by professors in the University of Utah: "There is almost no relationship between the grades a student gets in medical school and his competence and success in medical practice." Why the obvious should be so belabored is not always clear, but it is always pleasant to have ordinary sense confirmed.

The *New York Times* (Feb. 19, 1967) cites words from a committee of the National Education Association, leaving no doubts about their conclusion. The report card is "the sick man of education . . . a cramping distorting system . . . a nuisance to good teaching and learning . . . an ant-pile of scramblers, fighting one another for the few positions of safety . . . No one reviewing a grade is able to move backwards and to unravel the single score into the original strands which serve to create it . . . a deterrent to real learning." A Denver paper, quoting further from the same report, adds: "grades now represent a potpourri of subject-matter achievement, pupils' rate of progress, class citizenship, work habits, attitudes of both pupil and teacher, neatness, administrative and community pressure . . . no two persons interpret a grade the same way."

We might now look into the philosophy of grading and the reasons for its vulnerability. Some four criticisms of grades are notably common; others, mentioned less frequently, are of at least equal importance.

Grades are inaccurate. This needs no proof to anyone who has been a student. No experience in teaching is necessary to confirm the charge. Teachers themselves usually will concede inaccuracy without hesitation, though they may be worried about possible alternatives. Not many, however, have applied the old rule: When in doubt, leave it out. Educationists and psychologists have provided evidence of a so-called scientific nature and students can cite countless examples. The same themes and term papers have been turned in repeatedly in successive classes, acquiring grades which ranged over the entire scale. Mathematicians, often said by outsiders to have an easy time with grades, have also ranged widely in grading the same work; and why not, since some look for answers and others for methods. Honest teachers all admit that the first papers read (graded) get different treatment from later ones, and that it makes a difference whether a paper is read before or after dinner. The conclusions are unanimous.

Though the so-called inaccuracy is really an accurate expression of the basic technique, believers in grades try to gain in "accuracy," meaning consistency in error. Overlooking the ingenuousness of student's minds, they ask highly specific questions. They join the "objective" group in the belief that there is only one answer to: *Is a straight line the shortest distance between two points? Yes* ( ) *No* ( ). Einstein would have said *no*. Half the students in a medical class, some because they were suspicious of the question, also gave a negative answer. The purpose in using only recitational questions, as is necessary in the multiple choice type, is in itself evidence that the grade can control teaching, a reversal of the proper order.

The criticism that grades provide a notably poor motive for learning is probably second among criticisms in frequency. It is also well substantiated. Efforts to win a gold star or a grade are by no means the same as those devoted to producing a solid piece of scholarly work. Only the most naive student or teacher supposes that the acquisition of grades is parallel to scholarly performance. Outsiders should be aware of this, and many are. I never learned to color those Christmas trees at age five because no one said anything about the art of coloring; the talk was all in terms of getting those gold stars. Students know this discrepancy well.

Medical students, with unusually varied backgrounds in schools, have had every step they took determined by their grades. They are masters of acquisition. The medical school is the last of many screenings. Usually twenty-two to twenty-six years old, they work together as a group for four years. By this time, most of them make sure of the grades, after which they study legitimately. Even in medicine, however, students who fish for the honor society, the gold-headed cane, or a subsequent post on the faculty stand out among their fellows who are politely avoiding antagonisms while underneath they retain personal independence.

So portentous are grades as motives that the charge is commonly made that students would not work without them. The accusation is not acceptable. The evidence clearly proves that most students work as well or better. This has been demonstrated in many trials, even when the shadow of grades in other courses taken at the same time offered temptations to concentrate on courses that "pay off." The popular honors scheme which "allows" selected students to take one or two courses without grades has not led to loafing in the open courses. If the school means business and the students know that loafing leads to trouble, the scheme fits all courses and students, not a selected group.

The accusation does raise a question of standards and discipline, however. The idea of removing the heavy threat of grades is to permit freedom in which to work, not in which to loaf. Students who make use of their opportunities, as most of them do, should not pay the penalty due occasional class-mates who work only when threatened with disaster or when given a bonus. Students who abuse their privileges do not belong on the campus. Unless the teacher, department, and school work together to make this both clear and real, drop-ping students who do not perform, no plan will be effective. Except for this, however, the accusation that students are lazy shysters out for personal gain, more so than you and I, is libelous.

Several years ago George Mannello, Jr., of Hofstra Col-lege, tried to find out how students responded to grades. As is necessary in a limited study, he divided a class in one subject. True, the spirit of testing was strong, creating a grading atmosphere. The class made a serious effort to set grades specifically to one side, and the participants were interested in teaching, which was both a help and a bias. The mechanical use of "accepted" and "unacceptable" instead of a grade merely substitutes relative words, but with only two symbols no scale is established.

To "Has your perception of the function of a test changed in this course?" over half replied that to them a test was a *diagnostic* instrument. Grading was deeply ingrained; the idea that the function of a teacher is to appraise was not rooted out in one brief trial. In spite of this, ninety-five per-cent of the class said that their concept of an examination had altered. Seventy-five percent thought that their "perception of the nature of grading" had changed. Students felt less

tension, a note-worthy effect of nongrading. The feeling of
security rose as the course progressed [respect and a belief
in integrity of the teacher have to be earned with each class;
they cannot be requested or assumed], cheating diminished,
and all points favored nongrading. The wording of the questions asked and a knowledge of the objectives of the trial
undoubtedly influenced the answers. Despite the limitations,
however, the outcome was consistent with observations made
from various angles on some thousands of students of six
radically different groups in successive classes during both
terms and many summers over a period of thirty years.

That grades, based on how well a teacher is pleased, do
not match meritorious scholarship is a third common criticism. A teacher of radiology once countered this charge by
saying that he had just given an A to a student whom he
could barely tolerate. The two were completely incompatible
but the student's work was good. I suggested that the remark
that the work was good was a confession that he liked it,
and that he had used the relative word, "good," signifying
approval. "Pleasing the teacher" does not refer to blanket
approval.

We once had a student, before we dropped grades, who
managed to annoy everybody on the staff, though he was
capable and worked steadily. I had to take him aside and
assure him that he would get a B in the course, guaranteed
in advance, if he kept on as he was but left the staff alone.
He got his B, duly earned for that matter, with no more com-
plaints. The lesson probably helped him elsewhere, too. But
we liked what he did in our course. It is possible to have
conspicuous personal biases and still appreciate a student's
talents and efforts.

A student who faces a dozen or more different teachers
every term is obliged to please individuals who differ both
in subjects taught and in personal qualities. He needs his

grades. Pleasing teachers is an unscholarly game. If scholarship alone were in question, provided he had the talent and made the effort he could satisfy all his teachers with no trouble; but pleasing the teacher is a broader task, an unreasonable one.

Teachers do not agree on what constitute virtues or faults. During the twenty years of operation of a board which recommended promotions of medical students the records showed that the names of a third or more of the graduating seniors had been considered by the board at some time during their four years. Not all were discussed relative to probation or dismissal, but the value of an old rule in medical schools was clear, one once followed by many a current practitioner: keep your own counsel, do not make yourself known, and keep busy. A student who stands out is sure to make a hit with some of his teachers; and he is as sure to run into trouble with some. This will inevitably appear, under disguise, in grades, if they are used.

Agreement as to students who are deserving is the exception rather than the rule, and is necessarily meaningless when it occurs only by chance. Choosing a term in which we offered no course for the particular class, I once investigated the votes for honor students. Five departments had made nominations from a class of some eighty students. The practice was one followed every term. The departments had been asked officially to nominate candidates for honors, any number they chose, with no pressure applied. One stringent department had put up only two candidates and a generous department had turned in a dozen names.

In a previous example we found that nearly half the members of a unified class raised doubts in the minds of one or more teachers during four years of advanced work. In the present case the votes were for honors, those approved rather than doubted. The names submitted by only five departments covered a large portion of the class also. Some student could hence collect five votes. Even a skeptic might expect one smart fellow with a favored personality and appearance to get a unanimous vote. The fact was that no one got five votes, nor four, nor even three. Two students, neither of whom our department would have nominated, got two votes. The rest were nominated by one department.

To suppose that this outcome was due to inexperience or to teachers not properly acquainted with students and the rituals of grading is not reasonable. The five departments included both academic and clinical groups. The voters had not only the usual classroom evidence but also direct contact in laboratories or in the clinic. The voters had had extended experience in schools both as students and as teachers, and the experiences with people that medical training affords in addition. The clinical departments had devoted teachers as well as practitioners. This is not an error. It is not an extreme example selected to illustrate. It is not abnormal. It is a normal expression of facts. Pleasing the teacher fortunately means that we cannot please all of the people all of the time. Those who try may find that they please none.

Four common criticisms have been mentioned, inaccuracy of grades, the wrong motives that they provide, the need to please teachers, and the lack of agreement in general estimates of merit. Other significant criticisms arise.

One of the most cogent of these relates to the essence of teaching itself. The need to get grades discourages far more students than it stimulates. A reply to this is sometimes given: that it is unwise either to belittle the discouragement that life will inevitably offer or to give sticky praise for encouragement. Life is discouraging, and discipline has to be learned, it is true. Undue protection of students is poor teaching. And, though the essence of good teaching is to encourage students to put forth their best efforts and make the most of their talents, extremes of praise may offer happiness at the expense of considerable harm. Balance assumed, encouragement nevertheless is the essence of teaching.

A sympathetic class once agree to an explained vote on: what happens to you personally when you get an A and when you get a D, and how are you affected when your roommate gets an A or a D? The applause given A's because they were encouraging was almost nil, but the feeling that low grades were discouraging was pronounced. One student, perhaps fishing for an expected answer, said that a D stirred him to added efforts. The personal interests were high, but interest in the roommate's grades was limited.

Another major criticism of grading which gets almost no attention is also significant. Grades serve as masks behind which teachers can hide. Nowhere outside of schools do we have autocratic rule equalling the authority granted teachers over students. A teacher can record an F opposite a student's name and leave on a summer tour with no questions asked. He need not explain to the student nor to his chief. Students may complain but, if they gain any hearing, it is a private and one-sided talk during which the teacher juggles figures this way and that. Understanding of the subject is not discussed. The authority all rests with the teacher. The student is obviously biased in his own behalf, even if he is right. The teacher is thus assumed to make no mistakes and to have no biases, an unlikely postulate.

This authority provides so solid a mask that teachers who read papers with care cannot be distinguished from the skimmers. Teachers are guided by any factors they choose, to which must be added many that they fail to recognize or admit. They may decide on grades by intuition or by computation. When they have cast their decisions they walk off without being called upon to say why they made their choices or, if so, without producing anything but trite and general answers. Though this creates a most embarrassing vacuum for deans and students, it affords peculiar comfort to the teacher who hides behind the symbolic mask of six letters of the alphabet.

Students who are curious might try taking one of their graded papers to their teacher, one with a "96" on it rather than a "76" so that a defensive stance will not be assumed on either side. Let them ask the teacher what was liked about the paper and watch the teacher fumble with generalities. If he is a chronic grader, the teacher will never squarely have asked himself that question. Those who grade acquire a special ability to scan a batch of papers, jotting down marginal figures but using no helpful words. On the lookout for a few key signs, they barely skim the paper as they grab figures almost out of the air. Teachers who read with care are forced to keep their minds on a few salient points as they seek a goal of unattainable and inappropriate consistency. These are the pedagogic fantasies which foster multiple choice examinations and admiration for that word *objective*. The procedure is consistently in error. Examinations and themes get a standard type of reading, not necessarily slipshod but completely missing in all opportunities to note how a student is thinking and to help him personally to improve.

Another significant element in the criticism of grades concerns the fact that they foster black and white teaching. Academic life is pure gray. The point is basic. To attain any semblance of measurement grades have to be based on opinions of answers and performances, presumably as set against what someone regards as ideal. Just as the multiple choice test calls for the selection of the single answer called acceptable, an essay question calls for a discussion which someone judges to be acceptable in some degree. Scholarship itself, however, is *pure* gray. Pure gray differs from *indeterminate gray*, which refers to man's tendency to vacillate, to his penchant for indecision. Under the pure gray of scholarship, virtually all topics are granted impersonally to have various phases, each of which deserves fair consideration.

With ticklish subjects, such as religion, history, or its cousin, political science, the opportunity for bias is monumental. A worthy scholar will accept the multiple doctrines with little concern over his personal opinions of them, and will study and present them impartially. Society, when it accepted him for his position as a teacher, expressed faith in his scholarly outlook. If he is worthy of this faith, he will never indicate his personal biases. We have such scholars. Their students, left wing and right, Catholic or Mohammedans, remember their courses with pleasure. We also have teachers who use their positions to capitalize on biases, using their authority and their captive audiences of inexperienced young persons to indoctrinate. So long as we believe in a free society, why society should defend these persons under a banner of self-styled academic freedom is not easy to understand. For our present purposes, however, it is enough to point out that scholarship is basically pure gray, a status conflicting with the dogma which grading helps to invoke.

That grades flatly insult students is another difficulty which seems strangely to pass unnoticed. To label a student's sincere effort *D* and walk off is hardly a gracious act. This is the true insult, offered by one who sets himself up as a superior being with an unlimited right to act. Some years ago an article of mine about grades was published under the title of "To Grade or Not to Grade" (*Journal of Higher Education*, 23:264, 1952). The article was submitted under the title "To Grade or Not Degrade," but the editor changed it without comment. The fact is that our present teachers came from classes similar to those that they face. They are lucky if they came from the upper half in intelligence and talent. There is proof that they do not all come from the top decile by grades. In itself this should be enough to cause learned professors to doubt the efficacy of grades!

The insults are more subtle, as a rule, than the direct approach implies. By common agreement, *C* is a fair average grade. This symbol is sometimes scrupulously applied to seventy percent of every class, or it may be used more loosely. Yet everyone makes a constant effort to find his place in the sunlight. The attempt is noteworthy on college campuses, where the prime duty is to help each student to find his place in the sun. Any ranking procedure is bound to leave only one person in the warmth at the top, a fact which once again casts doubts on the propriety of the ranking procedure. The only possible way for every person to find his or her place in the sun, however humble, and most niches are fundamentally humble, is to help each to find a spot which fits personal talents, efforts, and preferably taste. No other answer is reasonable, except under an autocracy so well exemplified on campuses.

True, the world is full of ordinary persons, many of whom are sorry for themselves, sure that they are geniuses stifled by Fate. This is mere natural stuffiness, not to be condemned but not to be accepted, either. We all take plenty of *C* grades, the label of mediocrity, in the form of failed promotions, unaccepted art, missed blue ribbons, rejection slips from editors, tax laws, lost ballgames, and rebuffs from those close to us. This is normal.

Beyond these, however, we require some niche in which we can feel reasonably useful and successful. The bootblack, proud of the shine he gives you, stands head and shoulders above the business man who, instead of taking pride in the service rendered, is sorry for himself because he did not get the grade he wanted from his teacher, society. He had a business and it was accepted, indicating service rendered; if, by having done so-and-so, his service would have been better, another year is coming. The service is the legitimate goal.

With students, whose primary occupation is going to school, no chance to find their niches appears under teachers who stamp them several times a day with the label of mediocrity, the C. This is a serious form of insult, a deliberate destruction of the dignity of fellow human beings who will be next year's neighbors. In effect, the C says "You are most ordinary among *us*, the academic elite."

The grading of apples or cows at the county fair does no harm to anyone. The apples cannot care and the cows do not. The owners may fuss, but the fair is accepted as an athletic type of event, a competition in which everyone knows that vulnerable judges rule. My apple may be best to my taste or it may sell best, but your apple gets the blue ribbon. That is your good luck, and we had a good time anyway. That is hardly comparable to having a powerful authority judging you constantly, coming down on you, a person with feelings, with a C after every move. No one can welcome such working conditions. Students, obliged to try, do remarkably well. Would you expect a housewife to prepare a complicated dish under the eyes of a critic who stopped proceedings to put a stamp of unexplained approval or disapproval on each move? Would it not be likely that labor unions might have something to say about employees who were at the mercy of eagle-eyed supervisors who put down little black marks of mediocrity against the names of over half the workers from hour to hour?

Ultimately, we return to a consideration of grades as awards and rewards, as threats and punishment, and as misleading and artificial moves. That fear and incentives derived from greed undoubtedly provide motives for many of our moves is true. This, however, is a weakness to thwart, not a prop on which to lean. Even the most hardened skeptic must grant that many of our moves are made for worthy motives with true warmth and generosity, true desires to learn, and true wishes to serve.

The final word comes from those who seek to acquire a balance, placing them between the cynic, who sees only material motives, and the idealist, who with the attitude of a Pollyanna is blind to crass materialism and sees worthiness in all motives. Members of these two remote parties can agree, if they will. We do not have to ignore realities and materialism; worthy motives may be considered without giving them exclusive rights. If we will admit this truth, the educational path will be clarified. Scholarship can lean toward proper motives and away from crass motives without ignoring the places each takes involuntarily at times.

THOSE IN FAVOR OF GRADES, and the ayes defend their cause vigorously, range from conservative upholders of the status quo to docile conformers to custom,
from pragmatists to those indifferent to teaching, and from
the emotional rationalizers to sharp debaters. Those who
oppose grades cannot afford to overlook the differences
among those graders who are really interested in teaching.
From a teaching standpoint, the defenders fall roughly into
six definable groups: the disciplinarians, the authoritarians,
the benevolent, the politic tacticians, the tabulators, and the
escapers.

A first attempt to take positive action to eliminate grades
is sure to be bafflling because the opponents present
diversified attitudes. In any prolonged argument, the original
opponents will be joined by others, each side augmented by
persons who seize the opportunity to join one faction or the
other for reasons of their own, not necessarily related to the
original debate. G opposes H, but soon a, b, c, d, e, f, G is
arrayed against H, i, j, k, l, m, n. Raise objections to grades,
and certain teachers will rise in defense of them without even
considering other possibilities. Having looked at some of the
criticisms of grades, we should also look at the defending
groups.

The DISCIPLINARIANS see in the removal of grades the loss of a tool needed for the control of students. Every one hundred students will include several students who do not work or who are flagrantly inept. Several may be talkative, antagonistic, mischievous, or independent, disturbing their classmates and the teacher. In untoward situations disciplinary measures may be necessary. The need for discipline often gives rise to an assumption that students work better when the fear of consequences puts them under pressure. It is easier to lie in bed on Sunday morning than it is to get up and go to work on Monday. The use of threatening methods in teaching becomes a philosophy of the disciplinarians.

The threat of an F or a C unquestionably stirs a response in students. One does not wish to fail; another, after a scholarship, does not want a C. Assurance that the teacher can and will give these grades, if he chooses, naturally causes students to make every effort to avoid the difficulties. The induced fear accounts for many an act of cheating, out-guessing the teacher, plagiarism, fraternal advice, and all the tricks used to get grades. Threats offer an incentive not to learn but to avoid trouble. In theory, the principle is directed only at the few students who work only when threatened, but the sensitive and really able student usually feels these threats even more than those who deserve such treatment. The practice of disciplinary grading overlooks the great majority for the sake of a few, and those perhaps worth little attention. The disciplinarian is negative. The archetype of this group in all honesty believes that all of us work only because of the fear of consequences, far too inclusive a faith.

The next group, the AUTHORITARIANS, bears some resemblance to the disciplinarians. The disciplinarians are the arrogant Prussian officers; the authoritarians are the pompous town officials. One is proud of the power of force, the other of his superior authority to favor or deny. In this group of teachers appear the mice, who go into teaching because nowhere else can they expect such authority. Were they in a tax office or clerking in a store, they might be disdainfully officious. In the teaching world the authority over students is much greater than that of a clerk. The title of teacher or professor, plus the label of savant based on special knowledge of the subject taught, add to the feeling of authority over students.

To this authoritarian, grades are major factors in his authority, for he feels, perhaps unacknowledged or even unseen, that their removal would leave him in an unenviably vulnerable position. Even though he may realize that this vulnerability is warranted, he is unwilling to give up the symbols which provide considerable calcium for his backbone. He supports his case with the plausible argument that the teacher, with experience and advanced knowledge, is employed to teach, thereby granting the position of authority.

The answer to this group lies in its own vulnerability. In itself authority is neither desirable nor welcome. It should not exist, but of course it must. Under realistic demands just how authoritative the position of the teacher should be depends on a number of factors. Authority should be zero when not needed, which is a large share of the time; it may have to reach a high point when a fractious student needs to feel indisputable authority. But the right to use grades at will makes a point of authority. To rest on authority instead of attending to the realities of the problems of teaching, which is what happens with the archetype of this group, is to use grades to substitute control for teaching.

The BENEVOLENT group of supporters of grades may arouse feelings of warmth. They may also annoy with cloying stickiness. Benevolent teachers are the ones who see only good in all the dear young people, and find Dennis, the Menace, utterly charming. Students who are undeniably lazy are excused (they might be ill or have problems), mischievous students get the boys-will-be-boys soliloquy, slow students find their hands held in saccharine pity, students with insignificant successes are praised to the skies, and everything is just lovely.

These warm-hearted but misguided and unrealistic teachers find in the upper register of grades a special appeal. Removal of grades, which can remove a threatening weapon, can also take away a potent means of praise. Teachers in this group prefer to give only *A* grades. They spread around a few other grades, this with furrowed brows. Other grades are painful. Unwittingly, benevolent teachers are admitting that only by a spread can their *A's* have any meaning. Such teachers live in the clouded heights of high grades, honors, dean's lists, cum laude, scholarships, and lavish praise. When looking at students who do not deserve praise they are partially blind, just as the disciplinarian fails to see or takes for granted talented students. The facts speak for themselves. The support of grades on the ground that they permit benevolence is inadequate and improper. Reasoned benevolence has a place in teaching, but praise does not need grades, under which every blessing is impersonally relative and steps on those who do not have it. Fitting praise, because it becomes personal and specific, is helped by the absence of grades.

Practical allies to the benevolent group are the POLITIC TACTICIANS. They use benevolent grades in a calculating manner. An eminent medical teacher, responsible for major courses, was a typical politic tactician. He seemed strongly compassionate, but over the years it became clear that he was well aware of the consequences of his acts. An emotional idealist at heart, at the moment his praise was sincere, but he knew well what it meant. His award of gifts was guided by a knowledge of what would happen.

Students he liked and praised were about to become physicians, to join medical societies, to decide in his favor for internships, and so on. But his charity was consistent, for he turned in only one student for disciplinary consideration over a period of two decades. That student, a senior about to graduate, was reported ten minutes before the final meeting for the year held by a board that recommended disciplinary moves. The complaint claimed neither poor scholarship nor unethical behavior. An act of honest independence on the part of a student who did not like the tactics of a sticky political benevolence annoyed the politic tactician. The board somehow overlooked the case and the student became a successful and able practitioner.

To the politic tactician grades are portentous aids in awarding approval to favored students. Such teachers express a superior sort of interest in what they claim to be the "top ten percent." Some blithely admit that they are not interested in nine students out of ten, not only in itself a shocking outlook but, inadvertently, one which allows no denial of their particular choices for the top ten percent. Political teachers are present in most faculties, but no two of them agree on the students regarded as exceptionally able. The same differences in choice hold, fortunately, for future patients, neighbors, and customers. If we all saw and preferred the same qualities, the world would be a sad place.

Coming now to the TABULATORS, we encounter a group who may include mathematicians or those mathematically inclined. Since their training should mean that they are wary of improper conclusions, presumably mathematicians may be entrusted with grades, taking them for what they may be worth. Most teachers are not mathematicians, but they share with such specialists a fascination in numbers. Only when one knows what the numbers mean can the consequent limitations be clear. Figures can mean whatever one wishes them to mean. If numbers arouse chiefly an emotional fascination, as though they were snakes, they can be as dangerous or as inconsequential.

Grades in percentages or letters, used as symbols for numbers, provide possibilities for all sorts of manipulations. Tabulators like to think of students as units because then the juggling of names to arrange them in order of rank can be called objective. The list can be split into deciles or any fractions, and neat charts can be drawn. All varieties of comparisons appear attractive, however empirical.

As these words were written, the daily paper cited a chart which uses figures allegedly to demonstrate that the Intelligence Quotient and high grades were in a degree parallel, one more condemnation of the I.Q. test. Expensive surveys have been made to show that students who get good grades in high school are likely to get good grades in college. Advanced without blushing, this conclusion would have been predicted with certainty in two minutes before the investigation was started and at no cost by any high school student.

The answer to the tabulators lies in their basic reasoning. To assume that grading figures contain no information would be extreme, but the inferences made are rarely justified, and they do great damage. When a figure becomes a symbol for something it necessarily acquires the good and bad features of the thing it represents. If this representation is tied up with emotion or with a lack of precision, the figure, say a 76, appears to have far more than its real significance.

Applied to a student's work in English, for example, a figure has an accuracy which is obviously fictitious, and conclusions drawn from it become a menace to teachers, schools, and students. Mankind is fascinated by figures, but students and teachers are too complex to warrant the intrinsic precision of numbers. This is the basic reason for going from percentages to *A B C D E F*, in an endeavor to put the number of divisions small enough to be in accord with the possible degrees of accuracy. Another step was in order, not yet taken. The only way to prevent unwarranted conclusions drawn from juggling figures is to prevent the birth of the figures.

We come now to the ESCAPERS, teachers who favor grades because the symbols permit them to escape something. Some of them claim that they simply want to escape work. Any system other than grades requires thought; better yet, it permits thought. Ask a student to discuss the influence of T. S. Eliot on contemporary writers. Any grade assigned to the result becomes virtually impregnable. Ask a student what happens when an acid is combined with a base and grading may have less latitude, but teachers still are not teaching when they assign the grades whence come grade point averages and human fates in life, based on transitory recitations of facts.

Teachers are not often lazy, so we must look deeper. What the escapers seek really to avoid is not so much work as responsibility, a need to think and to accept the consequences of their decisions. Not even the teachers' own consciences hold them to account for the *C* assigned for reasons in part perfunctory and in part intuitive. The moment a teacher says "The student might have worked harder," however, he becomes vulnerable. He has stepped into the open to make a statement which he has to be prepared to support. Grades enable him to dodge this responsibility completely. Thoughtful escapists who support grades to avoid trouble see some of the dangers in this dodge. So few teachers have any direct experience with anything but grades, however, that the temptation to avoid trouble is great.

To the extent to which these six groups of upholders of grades can substantiate their claims, they should be heard. We do have to push ourselves to develop the essential self-starters. Fear of the consequences is not an imaginary consideration in guiding our acts. Teachers do need a greater authority than students have, praise can be legitimate and encouraging, politics is not so much worthy as unavoidable, and picking and choosing favorites goes on in all phases of living. Tabulators seek to improve judgments with tangible techniques, however obviously erroneous, and the hazards which escapers seek to dodge are real. Any substitute for grades must take these matters into consideration.

Can these points be met reasonably without resorting to grades? These symbols of approval and disapproval are used as means for attaining certain desired ends. Against this use are certain facts. Grades are artificial and indirect, they are in noteworthy respects a handicap to good teaching, and they lead to erroneous conclusions of serious import.

8. Describing Grades

To DISCOVER what is behind grades or possible alternatives several prejudices have to be overcome. Because they have never tried to find a constructive and practical substitute for grades critics have been handicapped. Sincere critics feel stymied by rules and by the difficulties of experiment when surrounded by courses in which grades are used. Hence they can criticize grades reasonably but, having little to offer on the positive side, their arguments get little attention.

Man has a strong tendency to establish two labeled camps; whereas the question itself, a proper ground for one camp, needs clarification. The decision is between two principles, between any system which involves comparative ranks and any or all possible substitutes. Unless there are substitutes which will overcome obvious faults without adding worse ones, only grading is left. If grading is a real barrier to good teaching, as it seems to be, condemning grading as not acceptable necessitates either a better substitute or proof that we can do without either one.

Probably the most common but oversimplified labels used to designate the two outlooks are the Pass/Fail system and the Grading system. This label for the substitute is a malicious blow against its consideration in any debate. The name favors those who prefer grades. As an alternative to grades, Pass/Fail sets a virtually unlimited latitude in acceptance of the work of students (passed), allowing only the most extreme decision against them (failed). The *San Francisco Chronicle* (June 1, 1965) says in an editorial: "Princeton University has inaugurated a program under which students may take one course each semester on a 'pass or fail' basis. Dean John Monro [now formerly] of Harvard sees this as a 'beautiful' means for enticing students into fields of learning they might otherwise avoid and says Harvard may follow suit."

Dean Monro saw in depth the adverse influence grades were having on teaching, but made this expedient remark on the evidence that "Fail" is virtually never used under such circumstances. This limited "permission" to take a nongraded course, which is widespread and not limited to Princeton, of course, is a clear indication that the removal of grades is generally regarded as a good educational move, whether admitted or not. Robert Bowen, who graduated from the University of California (Berkeley) in June, 1967, in mathematics, was interviewed by the *San Francisco Chronicle* (June 16, 1967): "'In the pass-fail classes, I learned much better than in my graded classes' . . . classes without grades allowed him to study for basic ideas. 'On the whole, I got more out of them,' he said." In all graded courses this student received only *A's* for four years.

Teachers are naturally unwilling to assign a flat "Fail" to students whose work they consider to be only questionable. Under Pass/Fail teachers are not permitted to question; they can only pass doubtful students or condemn solid sinners. Since students are likely to fall in the twilight zone of doubt, to force a teacher to include students about whom he has serious doubts with those whom he likes (Passed) seems out of order. Realizing this, a voting teacher is inclined to vote not so much for grades as against so drastic a substitute. Grades restrict him to the use of six ill-defined symbols; the alternative would restrict him even more, to two unmodified opinions of final judgment.

Attempts to circumvent the difficulty by the use of semantics have been at times ludicrous. A recent suggestion claimed that the prejudice against a *C* might be overcome if the grades were all moved up by definition. The "*C* = fair" became something like "*C* = entirely satisfactory." But the "*C* = fair" is generally understood to mean that *C* is not marked by any special depth in understanding, talent, effort, or anything else. That is the trouble with it.

A triangular scheme has been presented, possibly far-fetched but at least reasonably workable ("Triangular Grading," *College and University, 43* (1968), 143-149). This system divides the uses of grades functionally into three parts: (1) to serve as awards or punishments, as stimuli and guides in teaching; (2) to indicate degrees of merit in performance, a rough measure of ability and application; and (3) to estimate future promise, perhaps the most significant use, since what is done is done and what happens next, college, graduate school, scholarship, or perhaps probation, is paramount. Since these uses are only slightly interdependent, a single grade cannot possibly serve to meet the uses commonly attempted. By using *A B C D E F* separately for each one of these uses, however, some progress is made. An *A C B* grade would mean that a teacher could at least imply by his vote that he thinks that this student warrants full encouragement despite a rather ordinary performance, in which case his future would probably be rather good.

Triangular grading is a suggestion made as a concession, for it does not meet the principles of nongrading squarely. It does put a touch of reality into the use of a set of symbols which has become deeply ingrained.

The Pass/Fail suggestion arose once in our school but encountered objections because of its lack of flexibility. The discussion switched to Clear/Not Clear at the suggestion of an eminent clinician who caught the point of contention and was rather amused at the turmoil. The words were introduced and were used officially for some years. The marked advantage that Clear/Not Clear had over Pass/Fail lay in the fact that it put all students not cleared into a doubtful group for more general consideration without condemning them. To put "failed" or "not passed" after a student's name condemns him; to say "not clear" merely expresses a doubt which on further inspection may well turn out to be incidental.

If dismissal of a student does appear to the teacher to be proper, so be it, but the teacher has made his observations during his own courses, and he may more reasonably raise the question without casting his final vote until he knows some of the observations of others. The C = Clear and NC = Not Clear are still on the official records for students who attended over a period of nearly a decade. It has not affected their futures. The idea was workable, though it lost its effectiveness with some departments which still kept their own records in the traditional graded fashion. In these departments members of the staffs still thought in terms of grades and never caught up with the advantages which nongrading can afford to teaching. The only difficulties otherwise were the minor annoyances encountered by a school which dares to step a bit out of line.

The addition of a PH = Passed with Honors entered this system. One of the politic tacticians on the faculty, robbed of one of his pet strategic tactics, started it. Failing to see the difficulty that this introduced, the advising committee approved. Too many of them, never having caught the point, were still using private grades and thinking in grades under a nongrading opportunity. Several were interested only in teaching and ideally never thought about the damage or good done by any system. On learning that Passed with Honors was to be added to Clear and Not Clear, even freshmen and high school students from off the campus immediately noted what the voting majority of the faculty failed to see, thinking introspectively, that in principle this was a direct return to grades and the evils which had caused their removal.

Our interest here in this expansion of Clear/Not Clear is only to illustrate for purposes of clarity. For all their vaunted outlooks and fancied projections into life in general, honor societies illustrate this point well. They sometimes assume worthy functions. All of them include worthy persons. Nevertheless they have in common the same sort of relative approval that is behind grades. There is no denial of the theme song: We are good and, because we invite you to join us, you are honored. This theme is so definite that more than one student and some notable men have deliberately rejected offers of honors. This is a touchy subject, used here only to show what lies beyond simple relativity. *Any* group which elects you to its membership honors you, of course; societies are all "honor societies." Some groups, however, exist only to "honor," exemplifying the theme song in full measure.

Our real concern is with the philosophy behind the scenes. The basic problem is whether or not to accept the use of any sort of yardstick, percentage, or other empirical set of relative symbols to express points on an arbitrary range, spectrum, or scale to represent observations of alleged abilities of each student. We must either accept this principle of pointer and scale in some form, or prove that it is improper and find a better answer.

Excluding the important human equation for the moment, two detectable factors have militated in favor of grades, the apparent but misleading precision of figures and the propaganda which has made "objective" a saintly word, akin to "science" and hence impregnable. To try to deny that figures do appeal would be futile. To try single-handed to unmask the true features of objectivity, especially when used with reference to grades, would call for a long digression. The situation calls for specific treatment.

The range of scale used as a focus in qualifying students is based on comparisons, on the use of relative words and symbols both in mind and on records. Judgments based on observations are followed by personal classifications as good or bad, assigning faults or virtues to whatever is observed. This comes back to the vagaries of personal approval and disapproval. If a stranger remarked that your moral conduct was good, or more especially if he said that it was bad, your natural reaction would be to challenge him. Friend Joe, who is playing many roles as our illustration of a student, may have from me a feeling that "He could do twice as well but he is smart" and you may feel that "Though he doesn't get far, he tries hard," so we give him an A for opposing reasons.

To use a symbolism and a scale has many objectionable features, some of which have been discussed. To assume that the only alternative to the use of a range and a pointer is Pass/Fail is unfortunate. Education is only beginning to be designed in other terms. Thus far, sad to say, the alternatives seem to be based on variations in the use of a range or scale. The thought has been that the method of use is wrong, whereas it is the principle itself which is at fault. The scale of comparison is inaccurate; but to try to devise one which is more accurate preserves the faults of the scale. The grade provides wrong motives; to try to build better motives against the handicap which preserves the wrong ones can lead to no progress.

Though given sad twists at times, science and objectivity do have merit. If there were some way for students and teachers to be objective, to be so might be acceptable. No one has devised or is likely to devise a test of the blood which will reveal an unassailable measure of ability and perform-ance. Society has questioned the sanctity of blue blood, the red-blooded do not necessarily have intelligence to match, and the anemic are not much favored by employers.

How well the teacher likes the student or his work, promise, or personality involves so much of that complex person, the teacher, and so many qualities which have to do with students' assorted activities that merely moving a pointer on a scale is meaningless. We must somehow put aside the idea that "I like what Joe does" should be a matter of record for use as a legitimate guide in teaching and beyond.

In microbiology a favorite examination question we used for a while was "Define 'optimum temperature' for a bacterial species." The catch is that there is no answer. At one tempera-ture a given species will live longest, at another produce the most acid, at another multiply fastest, at another accumulate a maximum total population, and so on. Student after student, reared on relative words and grades, would answer: "The temperature at which it grows best." *Good, better,* and *best* are purely relative terms. They say nothing, but they allow you to read into them complex and personal inferences, and inferences are unstable items.

We can approach our goal only if we are willing to discard the scale altogether. Joe is going to make his own way in life, and he may never see Jane again. How Joe's efforts compare with Jane's really is of no consequence. Joe is Joe, and comparisons, the whole basis of the use of markers on scales, do not matter. Why compare Joe, who will perhaps pilot jets, with Jane, who might become a housewife or the first woman president? If we discard all the scales, each student can stand as a person, which each is, under any basic outlook in teaching.

The principle of nongrading is to detach one's self completely from the comparative viewpoint. Objectors will claim that this is impossible. From one angle they are right. In a semantic sense it is not possible to think or say something about Joe that is not relative. If I say his face is red, I imply a scale of color and place him on a range of facial colors. If I say he is ambitious, I imply that some are less so; and so on. In these instances, however, the scale used is linguistic and universal. It is not comparable to the use of a unique scale, my own, which I apply to members of a class if I use the classical relative symbols. In designating Joe's face as red I have no thought of Jane in mind, and you can infer nothing about Jane from the comment. Furthermore, I have not implied that anything is a fault or virtue.

In a broad sense, we are dealing with two opposing systems after all. A relative outlook or judgment is set against an open field of description. Shall we grade or shall we describe what we see? Teachers who will make the effort for a year or so will find that it is entirely possible to attain the feel of the descriptive philosophy.

It becomes possible to think of Joe as a person wholly apart from Jane. Even though they perform many of the same tasks, the outcomes appear as individual matters. What Joe brings to bear on the problem is not at all what Jane applies to it, even with the same problem and the same results. The descriptive outlook is as near as we can come to objectivity and science, if that matters. That is, the scientist squinting at his test tube is supposed to record exactly what he sees. In theory, but this is only in theory, he records exactly what is there; this is not possible, but he tries. The charge, heard now and then, that grades are objective and descriptions are dangerously subjective is a precise reversal of the truth. Both are subjective, but whereas one with modest success tries to describe objectively, the grader uses symbols to mask a higher subjectivity.

One reason that the descriptive outlook is not taken over easily enough to furnish more competition to grades than it does is that grading is so deeply ingrained. It has been part of us all our school lives. More than that, by nature we have a kinship with it. We live our lives within our own hides so, when I tell you about my broken back, you are impelled to speak of your back or a situation of which you have heard. A conversation of the ordinary sort is an exchange of personal likes and dislikes: "Oh, I didn't like it at all" is a common reply to "I thought it was wonderful." The point in teaching, and often elsewhere, is not in who likes what. The point is in the item itself, and what in particular about it is noteworthy.

The alternatives to grades involve this basic switch, from grades to a descriptive outlook, however applied.

FOR ALL THE DEBATES about freedom of speech that occur in academic circles, one phase is strangely unmentioned. Free speech is unequivocally curbed when the authorities or a consensus support a decree that teachers are obliged to speak about students for the record but they can do so only in terms of a highly restricted set of symbols. In unrecorded conversation teachers talk about students and students talk about them. Instructors compare notes, gripe about annoying students, express delight and dismay, and run the gamut of natural reactions. That some are more discreet or cautious than others does not disprove the existence of the human frailty. Discreet persons are more careful, less talkative, or perhaps more wary of influencing others, but they also observe.

Freedom of speech is much debated as a variously defined principle. Blood usually flows in arguments. Applied to the relationship between teachers and students, freedom of speech would seem to imply an official sanction to use the dictionary and the language to say, clearly and pertinently, just what each means when he speaks of the other. The descriptive technique refers to a shift from an enforced restrictive scale, range, or spectrum on which a pointer indicates relative position, good to bad, high to low, up to down, to the use of plain English to say what the teacher wants to express.

When one has once escaped from the grading ritual, in mind as well as on the records, it is surprising to find that colleagues do not object as strenuously to this restraint upon their freedom of speech as they do to lesser fancied infringements. Why they accept docilely a mandate which allows them to say only *D* about a student concerning whom they have strong feelings and an urge to give advice, quite possibly good advice, has been in part explained herein, but the phenomenon remains an anomaly. Faculties bitterly defend the rights of associates to make dubious comments on matters which are borderline as to scholarship, but they do not hesitate to spurn or ignore as important a teaching duty as the right to say freely what they mean about students. Not many proponents and users of grading ever seriously tried the benefits of free speech on this topic. This helps to explain the lack of reaction.

The first move in working toward a descriptive procedure is to eliminate relative terms from the minds, records, and acts of the teachers partaking in the shift. A lone teacher under a grading system can accomplish this and will find the move to be a step forward in teaching. To approach the change on a broader scale is better, however. A mixture of systems puzzles students. A unified outlook reduces friction.

The common scale of excellent-good-fair-passing-failed deliberately puts each student on a plane with others. Ask a teacher why he used a particular *A* and he says, with a satisfied air which implies an adequate answer, "because the work was excellent." *A* is the accepted shorthand for that comment. Instruct a new member of a staff that in his course he must refrain from grades and, brought up on them, on the first student's answer that meets his approval he will write out "excellent." In this process there is, of course, no gain whatever. Unfortunately, proponents of grades sometimes go no further than this toward analysis to satisfy themselves that their system is suitable.

If a teacher willing to inspect nongrading regards a piece of work as "good," he can hardly fail to see that a number of reasons might be responsible for that impression. The *reason* is significant, not his opinion. Who, after all, cares about instructor Jones' opinion of Joe's work? The school does care about Jones' observations, however, because they are significant in difficult decisions. The dean has to decide what to do about Joe and depends on Jones' information. He does not want Jones to tell him what to do; he wants Jones to tell him what happened. The dean has to decide what to do in a situation which he and the student are facing.

The change from a personal judgment based on comparisons with other students to an individually specific descriptive outlook, in mind and on paper, is within the power of those willing to try for a reasonable length of time. The change destroys nothing which grades provide except the more serious objectionable features which grades inject into teaching. The teacher still votes on students who encounter difficulties, but he is asked for his evidence, in words. Whatever person or group makes the administrative moves has a basis for deciding what should be done.

The teacher worked with Joe. It may be that Joe should go on probation, but should he? Not the teachers' judgments but their evidence may decide the issue. If several teachers vote for probation, that could be his status; but some authority has to issue the penalty and needs more than a count of votes to do so. If he merely counts votes and uses a book of rules, the system is convenient enough but it is hard on the victim and his friends.

When asked why, in words, they voted for probation, teachers who feed grades into computers are embarrassed and give routine answers like this: "Well, he got 52 in his first midterm and a *C–* on his term paper, and this 78 on his final doesn't bring him up much." This tells nothing to the man who has to take action. There is no meat in it, no teaching, no real help for him or for the student. The so-called objective system defeats its main objective, which is to teach.

Consider for a moment a dental student learning to prepare a gold crown. A teacher may stand by. Due to a break in technique the crown does not fit. The patient is naturally disturbed. The teacher could offer advice or he could put down a *D* in his little black book and walk off. The student is not interested in the teacher's opinion of the effort, in this case probably equivalent to his own opinion, but frowning repairs nothing. He rather desperately wants to be told just *what* is wrong, not *that* it is wrong. The mental response of the teacher should concentrate on the student's progress and thus on his relation to his task: "He will have to carve a new model." To think introspectively "He is clumsy and I will record that I think his work is poor" is a waste of teaching opportunity.

A student wants to know what is wrong with his work, not what the teacher thinks of it. A student in English can do nothing with a *C–*, a questionable opinion only of weight relative to others who do not interest him; but he can use informative guidance that will help his English. Ask a medical student how he feels about teachers who mark him down for spelling or, for that matter, for a medical error, instead of correcting both, pointing out the trouble.

To get rid of the relative words, following a natural inclination to use such words as substitutes for grades, it is necessary to practice the use of the language. Description requires thought and a fluent usage of words comes only after a little practice. Description is a new dimension, a shift from the imaginary geometry of projected planes to the encompassing realism of spheres, an advance from the simple shifting of a pointer up and down a scale to the pleasures and privileges of free reason.

The first active step is to learn to think as objectively as possible. Likes and dislikes are to be discarded; they are to be replaced by specific observations.

The next step hinges on a sharp question: When do you make these descriptive observations? The answer is as direct: When you can avoid it, you do not make them at all.

To pull out a notebook and put down an objective description, for example, that Joe, in response to a question, forgot to mention malaria, would serve no purpose. The act would drive Joe into a nervous state and the information would serve no purpose. Teaching is a process which takes place between teachers and students, in which one is supposed to help the other to advance in understanding, moving from basic factual knowledge to such wisdom as may be within reach. This process has to have the foremost position at all times.

One of the greater evils due to grading is that the practice turns teachers into appraisers, analysts, and inspectors, rather than the guides and counselors they should be and perhaps prefer to be. It is difficult for some teachers, supported by the grading practice, to steer away from the attitude of constant carping or criticism and to change to an observant attitude. To those teachers to whom encouragement is all, even when it is out of place, the curbing of sympathy may be troublesome. The only safe role, however, is that of a spectator. The critic, natural analyst, and the booster, all of whom use grades easily in accordance with their personal estimates, are automatically put on guard continuously against their natural urges, if they try to attain a fair degree of impartiality necessary for description.

With a descriptive attitude on the part of his teacher, without censure, praise, criticism, or encouragement, Joe emerges clearly as a person, unlike anyone else in the class. This is his true status. Joe has problems which only he can solve, but help is possible. Not much of this help calls for any record. The thought of a record, of its existence is a distraction and a handicap to both Joe and his teacher.

Persons, especially teachers, who cannot attend a movie, observe a show window, or speak of a person without exclaiming at length how much they like it or do not like it are to be pitied. They could say that Steiger seemed to live his part, that the color scheme was attractive, or that the neighbor was sensitive on that topic. Their ratings are unimportant. Ratings, without saying anything impose decisions on others. Even good friends, concerned over each other's preferences, do better with descriptions than with judgments. Life and teaching are smoother and more relaxed for teachers who succeed in reducing the attitude of relative rating to as low a level as possible. They can accept Joe as he is and leave him better than he was with only incidental and occasional personal judgments.

Administrative records have to show that Joe has passed his courses. Some information as to why the teacher thinks so may help when later inquiries arise. If doubts exist about Joe's work, not the doubt but the basis for it becomes important. Occasionally, therefore, a teacher can sit down and review members of his class, putting down pertinent points in words, the fewer the better so long as they say something. A class of students is composed of an assortment of complex persons. With a majority of the class a simple "O. K." would probably serve all purposes, but there is no way to predict whose name will arise for one situation or another.

As summaries, in this sense, grades are convenient but they say nothing, giving no reasoned basis for individual action. The only way to get at a useful and logical summary is to let nature take its course with teachers all the term. They can then concentrate on teaching, as they should. At the end, they can note salient characteristics which, during the course, have floated to the top. If the milk of human kindness during the course does not go into the cream separator until it is all pooled in the tank, the cream of the significant characteristics will appear at the small spout.

Sometimes this descriptive point of view centers around particular activities, such as examinations. Examinations bring the scrambled daily feeding process of heterogenous elements into a degree of unification. Let us assume an open question, one which calls for some thought and articulation, and suppose that a teacher approaches Joe's paper with curiosity and without preconceived ideas as to what is expected. At the moment Joe is it; what other students do is not in mind.

Reading the paper, the teacher picks up an error (corrected), a bit of twisted logic (indicated why), a bit of positive misinformation (scolded and told that, whereas missing information can be filled in, inadvertent misinformation which is carried away and retained becomes dangerous), and so on. Help will serve the writer of the paper; grades will not. At the end of the reading a summing up might read, "Full of information but you fail to put it together usefully." These eleven words can go on top of the paper and be entered also in the record book. A more specific and detailed summary is in order, if the teacher is willing, but that is between the teacher and Joe. It is personal and belongs at the end of the paper, never to be recorded and to be read only by Joe.

Note that, though the recorded summary is brief, for practical reasons, it does try to say something. It is not critical in the sense of censure and praise. There is nothing to invite Joe to feel superior or inferior to his classmate, Jane, nor is that any of his or the teacher's business. Jane, also a person, is a separate individual in the teacher's mind, in Jane's mind, and in the minds of those around her.

Experience with a descriptive system soon indicates that all comments and records should include the name or initials of the persons who wrote them. Joe is entitled to know specifically who made the comments on his paper. If this seems to defy what some think of as a cardinal rule of examinations, that all should be read consistently, so be it. The rule deserves defiance. The demand for uniformity arises entirely from the urge to grade. It is a central thought in calibrating the relative scales from which some persons find it so hard to emerge. Consistency is not a major point either in examinations or in teaching, as is evident in any inspection of similar courses under different teachers. If five teachers read several parts of examination papers, each should read in his or her own way, reasonable competence assumed, for agreement is not to be expected. Disparate grades or comments cause trouble, but under descriptive procedures consistency can be even fraudulent. More teaching is done with free efforts of teachers and students than when all are whipped into line.

Another factor requires the entering of initials in the record book, as well as on papers for students. Several descriptive commentaries for each student will accumulate by the end of a term. Whoever looks at them will see immediately that, though the words of each writer differ for different students, one member of the staff has used terms which are all but saccharine in their intent to encourage, another will be virtually brutal in criticism with rarely a word of praise, and the majority in between will still show personal idiosyncrasies. Simple observation is not easy; it just seems that way. Our disciplinary and benevolent teachers wear a new guise in their comments, one which makes it wise to consider them as part of their words.

Our staff once included a representative of each of these rather extreme outlooks. The sympathizer never put anything against a student in writing; but in degrees of praise the commentary ranged notably and suitably. Few students satisfied the other teacher, who was excessively demanding and exacting, and who in his way felt that he was baiting students for more work. Sometimes the discrepancies in comments provoked wild scrambles in the class, since the methods of teaching differed sharply, but students soon realized that teachers, like themselves, were individuals with their own ways. A tabulator type on the staff, who accepted nongrading only because he thought he must, was shocked at the words of the two teachers at far poles. Others were delighted, happy to have both kinds of teachers, for each filled an important niche. A staff of all one sort is going to miss many opportunities for teaching. Sensitive students will turn to benevolent teachers for guidance; tough ones will prefer the disciplinarians.

At the end of a course terminal comments might be: "A little slow perhaps but working hard and coming along. (MNO)" [benevolent]; "Can't keep up and will probably flunk out. (PQR)" [disciplinarian]; "Adequate. (STU)" [tabulator]; and, from the others, something like "Does not think quickly but is sensitive, persistent, and understands what he gets; will surely graduate. (VWX)." This series of descriptions, seemingly varied, is meaningful. It makes the student under consideration much more than a spot on a scale, especially if you know the writers of the comments. The commentators are as much a part of the story as are their comments.

The records just cited are terminal comments, summaries of *salient* characteristics made only for the record book. They differ accordingly from those which go back to students on examinations or papers, when help and guidance are still active. For a terminal comment a teacher may report a noteworthy sensitivity in Joe, but he would not thrust this upon Joe. In dealing with Joe the teacher instinctively realizes the need for care. On the other hand, outstanding sensitivity or slowness do belong in a descriptive record against an unlikely but possible need for evidence, and the final descriptions of salient features are made with this in mind.

At the end of the term, when all other data are in, teachers should have the privilege, also an obligation, of making comments which are primarily only for the record of the department. Those who, by conjecture, fear that such a practice will get out of hand have only to try it. They will discover that grades serve to mask in a way that words do not. The descriptive record is, after all, written, and it carries the initials of the writer. Unless reasonable judgment is used it can injure students, fly back in the face of the writer, or read as though it were part of a scandal sheet. Honesty and judicial decency are automatically introduced. This is certified by the records made by widely varied teachers on six different classifications of some thousands of students over a period of thirty years. Description reduces gossip and the comparing of notes. No member of the staff wants to see the comments of others before doing his own.

The procedure suggested, a way but not necessarily the only way to use the descriptive approach, is the outcome of a scheme which evolved with us over the long period of trial. The records contained a few lines of individual description in words about each student. The record books of graded students reveal batteries of figures, letters, and personally devised codes, each a struggle to say something with poor substitutes for words. Viewed as records, even without regard to teaching, in the aggregate graded records consume as much or more time than is required for a few descriptive

words, and with notably less usefulness. Graded, every symbol points to "I like it;" in the other case, every word points
to what named observers saw or thought they saw.

The final record may include three or four items entered
during the term, from half a line to two lines each, all of
which are known to the students. The final comments are
then added, made for the book by each teacher who observed
the students. Every word applies personally to Joe or Jane.
The total comments create a partial image of each student,
at least as he appeared to the department. Joe may finish as a
bit slow and he may stand out for his industry. Jane may have
a quick but erratic mind, and be classed as an academic shark
who spends too much time on extracurricular matters. These
and similar points are all custom-made, pertinent to the status
of the student as academically viewed.

10. Another Look

To STRESS ITS MAJOR FEATURE, the technique described, an application of a descriptive approach as contrasted with a grading approach, has been called "The Flotation Technique." First published in the *Educational Forum* (23:41-53, 1958), it has appeared also in *Improving College and University Teaching* (8:23-29, 1960) and in a collection of articles edited by Estrin and Goode, *College and University Teaching* (Wm. C. Brown Co., 1964).

In 1938 William S. Learned, Harvard, in his "The Student and His Knowledge" (Bulletin 29, Carnegie Foundation for the Advancement of Teaching), demonstrated that he had been one of the early observers to catch the intellectual off flavor in grades. He proposed as a substitute a rather complicated profile for students. In the usual simple meaning of profiles, the contours are held to a limited series of peaks defined in advance. With flotation, the necessary freedom permits concentration on the natural paramount qualities, however common or unusual. This freedom is significantly important for pertinent description, as well as for elimination of all consciousness of a defined pattern of appraisal which, if allowed to exist, is sure to hang over a teacher and affect his teaching adversely.

As this volume goes to press news announcements mention a five-year plan to "drop grades" at Yale, adding that they will use honors-high passed-passed-failed. Like so many alleged substitutes, this only paraphrases grading. Dr. Learned avoided this and sought description rather than ranking, with dubious success, but he did not pass the hurdle of schematic and predefined restrictions, also with the same old stress on appraisal.

The principle of "flotation" puts a practical note in the descriptive approach. The relationship between teachers and students is inevitably doubly human. Two persons are intent on one job, the student's learning. No one in his right mind can favor the model of a teacher which makes him an inspector who stands behind a rail, watches, and records judgments. The model would be fatal to good teaching.

A teacher who engages in free description only of qualities and characteristics which jump at him is not looking for features to describe or for characteristics which he can classify as virtues or faults. A term with Joe, however, enables a teacher to see one or more qualities which have floated unseen to the surface, as surely as the microscopic globules of fat rise in milk and coalesce to form cream at the top. The process is not and should not become other than involuntary and incidental. Joe stands out for his industry, for his laziness, or for some other special quality which is pertinent to his academic performance and talent. Usually apparent only by the end of the course, occasionally it appears quickly and thrusts itself unwittingly upon the teacher.

The tabulators and systematists like to reduce everything to a blank form. They are inclined to make use of the idea of characterization by preparing a chart on which they list a score or more qualities, some pertinent and some of doubtful usefulness. They then return to grades by giving each quality five or even more degrees of freedom, excellent, good, and so on. They expect every feature to be covered for every student by the use of check marks. This, of course, is worse than grading. It is again the scale, carried past the impossible to the point of absurdity.

Teachers with experience will have encountered this sort of thing. With twenty characteristics, only forty students, and seven degrees of freedom, as occurred on the last sheet I saw, there would be forty sheets, each with 140 squares, or 5,600 possibilities to consider. My suggestion, since we were under an administrative mandate to return the forms, was that we put check marks in at random so that the patent absurdity would take its proper place. This, however, was dubbed unethical by my unduly ethical staff, so they took over the blanks. The tabulator who invented the forms had some happy days of toying with the useless results from assorted departments and that ended the matter.

Once "flotation" squares off against this sort of tabulation, the trouble with charting becomes immediately apparent. Under the principle of "flotation" the significant features float to the top and stand out. Even when the reports say that Joe is "Quiet; nobody seems to know him," the record gives some sort of definitive idea of how Joe appeared to those who worked with him.

The tabulator is misled on this. Joe is perhaps lazy. Everybody is somewhat lazy, so the chart-maker has an urge to fit this feature to all members of the class. By "flotation" perhaps Jane turns out to be industrious, so Joe and Jane stand out on the quality of effort expended. If a chart is used, however, most of the energy is spent in efforts to measure degrees of laziness for all other members of the class, in none of whom is laziness or industry significant, being neither high nor low. The process is not only monumental in scope and boredom; it obscures all the salient features in the mass of data. That Joe is notably lazy and Jane is industrious is lost.

How much useful information has been buried in the nation's files because of the present plethora of duplicators which make multiple copies too easy, no one will ever know. Successful speakers recommend that neophytes learn when to stop. Teachers of English spend time in advising about the beauties of concise writing. "Flotation" is a principle, one which recognizes the stopping point. It is especially applicable to descriptive nongrading.

Opinions that students have about grading or an alternative have had many exposures, a few of them recorded. On checking over my scars, I find several illustrations. The one that caused the deepest wound came from a high authority. Although he appeared to belittle grading, some of the weaknesses of which he recognized, he claimed that our school returned from Clear/Not Clear to grading because the students wanted it. This was not true.

The full story is too long for the present situation. There was an element of truth in the idea, however, which no doubt accounts for the assertion. The claim that students want grades was based on incomplete evidence, one of those bits which defy the "and the *whole* truth" fraction of the oath. We have already pointed out that both students and teachers can be quite happy and satisfied with perfunctory performances when the teacher tells the students exactly what he wants, teaches them exactly that, and then pays off as promised. This comes under maximum security, not under education. The high administrator who claimed that students wanted grades was unwittingly weighing this sort of routine teaching. Students fear some of their teachers. When talking about grades only occasionally with high administrators students realize that grades give them a chance, because they can meet specified demands. With the black-dog type of teaching grades make life easy. The few students interviewed now and then by administrators instinctively want to appear to advantage and to protect themselves.

At the time that the return to grades was in the air, a step which became inevitable after the politic tacticians managed to add "Passed with Honors" to Clear/Not Clear, two of us presented a question to the presidents of the medical classes of the second, third, and fourth years, all of whom had had a course under the "flotation" technique and had only C/NC on their records. Including no arguments either way, the question simply referred to the proposed return to grades and sought the students' preference. It was signed by two on the faculty who were both known to the students, one for grades and one against. The classes considered the question in their own ways. The results were overwhelmingly against grades. One class even voted a hundred percent against them by blind ballot. The influence these votes had on the vote of the faculty was of course completely negative. Papa knows best.

The same situation arose in a dental faculty, so far as a return to grades was concerned. In this case the opinions of students were not obtained, however, because several important members of the faculty vetoed a formal request that we first take a vote of students to see how they felt about returning to grades. The veto arose from the feeling that the faculty had the right of way, which would have been true without regard to the results of a poll. It was also politic, for the veto avoided the need to act in opposition to the students' vote, as the speakers clearly felt would be more than likely.

In view of these and other instances over a long period of trial, I feel personally that most students are basically against the use of grades. They know that a nongrading viewpoint cuts down the struggles against one another and against teachers, allowing them to study. True, a few proponents see in grades a chance to get ahead of others under competitive conditions. Quite likely a few students vote against grades to prevent just such activities, for that matter. The proponents often included those who would get the top grades which they felt that they deserved and might get, though exceptions occurred. Most of those most active in approval of nongrading were students who stood exceptionally well in terms of grades.

To be guided by votes of either the faculty or students is a wrong approach to the problem. Their votes furnish no more than indices of the troubles which might arise with a change. Since proponents and opponents take part in all proposals, the basis of decision has to be based on reasoned arguments themselves, in terms of right and wrong, seeking which one is preferable in accordance with fair play and good teaching. Otherwise the strongest talkers and those with something at stake take over.

The wide use of surveys and popular opinion polls has almost wiped the idea of reasoned right and wrong out of existence. To go along with popular opinion is not necessarily right nor democratic. Democracy does not mean that the result of a poll always shows the best way; sometimes it is the only way we have devised to settle difficult choices which have to be made, right or wrong. In our current problem, the search for right and wrong may properly take precedence over Gallup polls.

The popularity of the poll in part is perhaps responsible for the urge to reverse the grading procedure, with students grading teachers and their courses. This has taken all sorts of forms. In recent years several colleges have published volumes of opinions and put them on public sale. The *Yale Daily News* not long ago published a paperback, at $1.95, with 164 pages of criticisms of courses and professors. At the University of California students have also furnished such "aid." These clearly are organized schemes to meet social demands which students find no other way to meet. Optimists, able to find gold because they ignore the dross, may note this favorable comment about one teacher: "The most important thing is that a great man has bothered to think about your paper and taken the time to write a valuable comment on it." Is it not remarkable that a simple act, presumably as much a regular part of a teacher's duties as anything he does, should be considered worthy of special favorable comment?

In one western university, polls by students on courses and teachers were sought by administrators and were used as partial grounds for promotions. In Oregon a legislator made tax monies available, in attractive figures, as awards for members of faculties who won in various types of popularity. In theory, such awards are for merit in teaching, but fortunately "merit" has defied all definition. Students may have the rights to opinions, but the propriety of such collective judgments is distinctly debatable. Too many questions today concern rights, too few concern right. If we must use collective opinions rather than individual articulation, polls that consider the dangers should be invoked. The idea of appraisal by students can be at least realistic and understanding. The teacher may voluntarily ask for appraisal, but the request needs care.

To collect students' ideas, giving them a place to express themselves safely without later abuse of their data, is not easy. Oregon State University seeks to help the process by the use of two sanctioned appraisal forms which pertinently differentiate between the teacher's status (is he prepared, does he speak clearly, are his tests fair, etc.) and the student's personal feelings (has my interest grown, has this course contributed to my educational background, and so forth).

The drawbacks are those which lie in the use of forms for questionnaires. A plain sheet of paper would permit the "flotation" technique. Students would then record what struck them forcefully and drop the rest. The questions are too wide in coverage and draw forth no personally expressed comments.

Characteristics fall in the familiar form of the survey, calling for checks of "Excellent, Good, Fair, or Poor" for the teacher, or "Greatly, Moderately, Little, None" for the student's self-appraisal. Answers are directed, as they are in all forms, and items are too numerous. The committee of faculty and students which set up the questionnaire was carried away by its task of coverage and the main issue was lost. One can feel its minds groping to meet all contingencies instead of searching for cogent answers.

Such voting items as "I have improved in my reading comprehension" and "My regard for different points of view has increased" are certain to produce answers of little meaning. The forms have the drawbacks which faced the teachers who had to mark seven degrees of alleged perfection in twenty qualities for all students. Only one or two qualities are significant for any student or teacher in such situations, and some of these are certain not to be mentioned in the forms. They will be overlooked by the student thrust into the guided and pedestrian process of completing a form.

Though an atmosphere of criticism arises with little stimulus, an atmosphere favoring efforts toward good goals is surely preferable. Teachers often have to choose between two courses of action in their teaching. Either choice leaves them vulnerable to attack because of the loss of the virtues obtaining in the alternate choice. When teachers weigh appraisals themselves, they may rationalize but they need not face another's interpretations or, worse, insidious unrevealed misinterpretations. They can allow for valid but uncorrectable criticisms. Even the use of forms gets some good out of the move, it protects all without scandal, interpretations are in the hands of the proper party, and the votes of students, though unfortunately prescribed by a form, are personal rather than by mob influence. Note that this effort, like all such, despite tabulation seeks description, not rank.

A real tabulator in our school, who made a fetish of statistics, once persuaded his class to fill out opinions of various departments, courses, and teachers at the last class meeting of their senior year. Caught at this opportune moment, when they felt wise and safe, and were through with nineteen years in schoolrooms, the seniors went to work. The results were to go back to the man who sought them. This gift was equivalent to a box of dynamite or a contract with a syndicate for a gossip column.

On another occasion an administrator put the burden of guilt on the students, claiming that they got up their scandal sheet which he felt that he should permit. The evidence strongly suggested that he had provided some early hints himself. The results went to him and he kept them in his own file, revealing only what he chose to reveal and using the evidence as he saw fit, though he could not possibly know both sides of the points raised.

Grading of the faculty is no better than grading of the students. Those who want an eye for an eye might use the reversed grading of the faculty vindictively with some justice, but "two wrongs do not make a right." The atmosphere of criticism created by those who grade is not a good working atmosphere. Whether the teacher grades in the classroom or the students grade in the union building, the process is not conducive to learning. The main issue is a concentration on learning, taking the foibles of both teachers and students as they come, improving them a little here and there when opportunity offers but never allowing the major objective to be upset by these introspective almost morbid tactics. Grading is better avoided both ways. Description makes clear the fact that it has to be carefully and ethically used. If students must please their teachers to get A's from teachers and teachers, in turn, want A's from students, the situation becomes harmonious politically but most improper for progress and improvement. Equilibrium then levels off at the mediocrity of good fellowship, which is not equivalent to joint intellectual challenge.

The teacher who does not watch for specific observations of students, whether criticisms or approvals, while he works on faults he already knows that he has, does not deserve to be a teacher. Unless what he learns from others is individual and descriptive, it is valueless. Griping and flattery are grades again, "I dislike" and "I like." By whomever started and however managed, most of the appraisals by students have automatically sought appropriate, considered, specific, and descriptive comments. Students have not given teachers C– and B+ grades on a relative scale, within my experience, though such would not be surprising. What is surprising is that teachers choose grades when they could demand of themselves those appropriate, considered, specific, and descriptive comments.

11. The "Gifted" Student

THE REASON THAT GRADES are philosophically so readily accepted is that they have a hidden flexibility. They resist disapproval because the usual symbols, *A B C D E F,* are so transcendentally vague that each user or observer who considers them unwittingly puts his own personal interpretation on them. *A* signifies "excellence." This definition allows any teacher to lick his lips in pleasure because "excellence," though independently unique in each mind, means to each exactly what he regards as "excellence." As Humpty Dumpty tells Alice, a word means exactly what he wants it to mean.

Put your idea of "excellence" to someone in meaningful words, other than relative vagaries, and trouble begins immediately. To one man mental agility is a paramount indication of excellence. The next man, however, from his experience is skeptical of this. He regards steadiness and perseverance as the paramount signs of excellence. Genius is largely hard work. One teacher claims to be guided exclusively by the student's performance, but the next one says that a student who shows marked improvement deserves much more credit than those who perform fairly well as they coast along with little evident development.

This also explains why the shift away from grading or to a nongrading descriptive outlook is so puzzling to many teachers. Peace is pleasant. Since no one has to define his concept of "excellence," so long as we speak only of "excellence" one can hide behind grades and can be happy with his head in the sand.

We encountered earlier teachers who said that they were interested in only the top ten percent of their students. These are the teachers who, for example, will scorn freshmen and will consider their personal talents to be wasted on less than graduate students. Certain that they themselves are of that ten percent, they clearly regard themselves as aristocrats. Whether or not they belong in that exclusive bracket is anybody's choice. At least, inspections of the early academic records do not always verify the assumption in terms of their *grades* as students.

These men are class conscious. Self-assured because their status on the campus impresses them, they accept as peers only those on whom their personal blessings fall. Their idea of excellence is the genuine article and those who differ are mistaken. The idea that relative words have specific meanings permeates farther than this self-styled aristocracy. It reaches all teachers who believe in grades, each of whom feels confident about his own ideas of excellence or good and unwittingly assumes that the other fellow, unless he agrees, is a poor judge. In short, graders favor the "gifted" student.

This philosophy of personal definition, the use of a word such as "excellence" as a substitute for a nonexistent definition, fills the atmosphere of campuses. It appears among those who recruit students. It is used in accepting their credentials. Students who transfer from one college to another are likely to be told that they have not properly studied certain subjects already covered so they must enroll in the local courses. Graduate schools weigh colleges which furnish their students. All sorts of academic practices run the route of the gold star. Participants in education define "excellence" their own ways.

Descriptively considered, the "gifted" student has no reality because nothing is specified to define the opinion. No one can signify what special combination of characteristics meets general relative terms like "gifted." "Excellence" is selective but it does not select. The philosophy which supports the "gifted" student rarely picks out genius, and genius is far rarer than those so labeled academically. But let a student acquire a large collection of *A's* and he will get great doses of admiration, not only in the academic world but from hangers-on who, though they can hardly be blamed, accept the guile of campuses.

Should we oversimplify and speak of "performance" instead of "excellence" in an effort to give the concept of "gifted" a greater substance, we would gain little or no ground. The vagueness of relative terms continues to make efforts to define performance peculiarly baffling. Performance, usually referring to little more than the teacher's satisfaction in the degree to which a student completes assigned work, is surely inadequate to measure a student's mind, progress, and understanding.

A simple but unduly general scheme might help to keep a reasonable focus on performance. Since students who do not apply themselves are wasting opportunities, no matter how bright they may be, let E stand for effort. Then let T stand for talent relative to the subject, an element which is not part of teaching but is a gift which comes in all degrees. Performance, or P, becomes the result of the product of the two: $P = E \times T$. A great effort can often make up for a weakness in talent, and a pertinent talent along academic lines may allow latitude in the output of energy. The formula has a strange resemblance to *force* $=$ *mass* times *acceleration*,

or to the power in volts which equals the amount of electric-
ity times the resistance to its passage. This scheme does
equate performance with results, though it is at best a poor
attempt to give substance to abstract ideas. Performance,
after all, is only a small part of the story.

The philosophy of description appears to negate the
existence of the "gifted" student, a conclusion which is
patently unjustified. Unquestionably some persons have both
wider and stronger assortments of talents than others, and
some have higher degrees of any named talent than others.
Description, once absorbed, grants this. The descriptive
record may indicate that Joe has a high talent for athletics;
or it may ignore such a quality, since with most students and
courses the talent would not be pertinent. The record may
show that a dental student has such a poor eye for form that
his career is dubious. But for the future of a journalist such
a weakness in a talent is not noted or mentioned.

If observations are to be descriptive, talents have to be
specified. Once this is done, separating the "gifted' 'students
from the ordinary ones appears in its true light as undemo-
cratic, precarious, and asocial. This is not glorified theory.
It is demonstrated all around us by the subsequent lives of
students who were designated as "gifted" by teachers. No
doubt our tabulators would say that from those so labeled
more taxes will be collected per person than are taken from
those who were regarded as members of the ordinary group,
but exceptions are exceedingly numerous. Impersonal averages in such matters are distasteful and impertinent. Academic talent, as measured by pleasing teachers, is far from
being all-inclusive. Valuable within its narrow sphere, it cor-
relates somewhat with useful talents, but it is by no means
the comprehensive and sweeping talent that is often implied.

The right man in the right niche looks good but no man,
genius or not, fits in all niches, nor would such ability usually

have point. That the purpose of campuses is to turn out men and women of whom all can hold up their heads, if they find the right spots for their personal sets of talents, seems axiomatic. Though it is not always apparent, campuses do not exist so that admirers can select their own ideas of the top ten percent of those who come to them, the ones who, with the admirers, all too obviously hope to rule the world. If faculties are to condemn to mediocrity nine hundred students in every thousand, it is time to give said faculties F for described reasons.

The question of honors students among undergraduates was under discussion once in a seminar. The designation was defined as referring to those with high grades who might be allowed special privileges. The privilege at the moment concerned courses in which grades would not be used, as mentioned earlier. This is an interesting point of view to note from those who were even then regarding grades as the basis for selecting these same students. When my turn came to express an opinion, I welcomed the special privilege and then suggested that the purpose in mind should properly make all students honor students so they could partake of it, not a bad idea without calling them honor students.

The extremes to which the concept of excellence may be carried is illustrated by committees which recommend awards and scholarships. Wealthy persons, believing in education but not especially familiar with the workings of a campus, bequeath money for scholarships. They may or may not specify certain qualifications of those to whom they want the scholarships to go. Without any specifications, donors are at the mercy of the "ten percent" aristocrats, who are sure to be well represented on scholarship committees. Each sure that his concept of the "gifted" student is correct, the academic body is likely to select a recipient whom the donor would not have chosen.

Donors who have in mind a special purpose thus stipulate the conditions of the award. It shall go to sons and
daughters of war veterans, it shall go to students from the
donor's geographic area, it shall go to students whose records
in science are exceptional, it shall go to a student from Africa,
and so on. Such stipulations are frowned upon by scholarship committees because they restrict the choices of those
academic bodies. By law, ethics, and reason the donor has
a right to stipulate what shall be done with his scholarship.
The attorney for the school and its trustees or regents agree
to this when they accept the funds and the responsibility.
Since schools rarely turn down money, the stipulation becomes legally and morally binding. You would never discover this obligation from listening to the ideas of the
"gifted" student expressed by a scholarship committee. Members of the faculty are sure that their ideas of who deserves
awards should be regarded as final. Papa still knows best.

The idea of a blanket of worth implied in an A, in *excellence,* in the "gifted" student, and in the upper-ten-percent
aristocrats reaches further than the classroom and the dean's
office. The populace, meaning parents, students, and citizens
at large, has been carefully coerced into acceptance of the
blanket idea.

In these days of tremendous emphasis on education
nothing could do education and its institutions more good
than to have society take it for exactly what it is, no less but
no more, either. Education is undeniably of great import; as
undeniably, it is not everything. The thought that academic
worth covers total worth is objectionable on campuses; in
society it is unacceptable.

At the most a high grade refers to a sort of general
academic proficiency or talent. Nobody, however grades are
rated, could reasonably maintain more, though the claims of
honor societies certainly imply that their members excel in

all directions. That not everyone who excels in his work wears a key is obvious; equally obvious is the fact that not all who wear keys are noteworthy in the niches they try to fill. It is not reasonable to suppose that academic excellence is equivalent to overall excellence, even if one grants that grades locate such, which they do not.

Yet descriptions meet these contingencies. Descriptions help to remove thoughts of the "gifted" student. There are many talents, unevenly distributed. If we must succumb to the urge to say that an ability to pass examinations, read books, or be proficient in certain special courses on the campus warrants a claim for excellence, on the assumption that such recognition will help morale more than it distracts from the work at hand, then let gold stars at least mean something definite for specific persons and tasks.

Nobel prizes are given only for the narrowest of performances, presumably backed by distinctive talent. The winning performance which led to the prize usually has far-reaching effects, a fortunate circumstance, though it suggests the presence of a strong touch of serendipity. We award medals for special performances but no one expects them to signify talent in all directions.

Alleged talent, even limited to academic matters may mean reasonable success in understanding the substance of several courses. It may mean exceptional application. It may mean an unusual preparation. Certainly it can signify a delightful personality which seeks and finds favor with most professors. That these indices, whichever one may dominate, are so often thought to cover more ground than they do can be explained only by paying dubious tribute to the propaganda used by our campuses.

In speaking of the pooling of descriptions, grades, or talents, as you may choose, we approach the administrative problems which link the campus with the outside world. To

the administrator, Joe is likely to be one of the faceless assemblage that registers yearly for the first time and appears
eventually in the black cloud at commencement. Between
these two events, however, Joe and his mates have highly
personal problems which, when they have to be viewed by
administrators, are definitely individual. When Joe's parents
visit the administrative office, perhaps in wrath, they want to
talk about Joe. His classmates and the cabalistic symbols
of the teachers do not interest them. Teachers are responsible
for administrative bases for decisions, so let us now sit with
administrators. They seek to carry out the dicta of teachers,
however judiciously.

12. Rules and Rulers

IN EDUCATION, an administrator is a liaison officer between hypothesis and reality. Teachers live with hypothesis. Convincing as their ideas are during the day, seeming to be fraught with reality, teachers are none the less destined and privileged to live in an ethereal world, the ivory tower, the realm of dreams. They are ordinary persons whom society employs to pitch the mysteries of their minds and the flexible sources of their energies against the problems of other human beings. They deal with alleged truths and with purported virtues and faults on which there is imperfect agreement. In the futures of students who leave them far behind teachers can never know what parts they may have played, if any. The administrator deals with students and teachers, and also with the realities of admissions, praise and punishment, other schools, parents, alumni and alumnae, and the public.

Outwardly, grades are designed more as aids in administration than as factors in teaching. They furnish a shorthand for recorders, a bookkeeping system for units needed for graduation, a basis for admissions, a key to honors, a tool for discipline, and a sort of coin of the academic realm which serves in assorted ways in educational transitions. Inwardly, grades are definitely something else. They are crumbs for the frustrated inhabitants of the pedagogic ether. Teachers guide many administrative acts through their grades. Were grades limited to more red tape to please administrators, however, they would have less than no standing with teachers. Obviously enough, this is not the case.

What, then, do administrators think of gradient scales when set against the possibilities of description? Much as they hate to make the concession, teachers admit that, unless the administrators are reasonably happy, there will be trouble. Looking over the many administrators under whom I have served, I am loath to generalize. Separation of administrators into three categories, however, may permit some broad conclusions.

The stickler species of administrator is an orderly fellow who thinks a school should operate as precisely as a bank. The books must always balance. Though this administrator keeps his book of rules handy, he does not need it because he knows all the rules by heart. At a moment's notice he can select one which proves his point, no matter which way he chooses to go. Granted, the combination of grades with a book of rules is a great boon to this type of administrator. Teachers who fear their ruling chiefs or whose minds work by rules consider this aid to be an argument in favor of grades. The rest may well wonder whether improvement rests on changing the grades, the rules, or this brand of administrators.

The opposite species of administrator puts the rulebook in the corner and lets it collect dust. He is a law unto himself. He is well aware that a rule can be found to support either side of any issue, if anyone cares; he does not. He is an autocrat. Like the monarchs of history, if he happens to be a wise, able, and honest autocrat, he becomes an excellent administrator, one whose portrait done in oils will grace the halls of the future. That is at least more than the rulebound administrator can expect.

Following the inescapable laws of equilibrium, the third species is between these two extremes. Administrators of this group know the rules but are more concerned with the intentions than with legal fencing over the interpretations of words. Knowing that every decision, good or bad, will meet with opposition, they figure that they might better try to seek right answers than to try to please others. They would rather be right than president, and they know that fair play is not always found by compromise or by a middle course; it may well be something that for the moment irritates both sides in the point at issue. Political administrators, who take the advice of the most powerful, are sometimes erroneously confused with those who seek right answers.

Administrators include presidents, chancellors, academic deans, executive managers, registrars, admissions officers, recorders, a number with strange titles, and the assorted deans of professional schools, one for each school, including the graduate school. Deans correspond to vice presidents. When the top brass wants to get rid of a task which is a nuisance, it appoints some ambitious member of the faculty to be a dean of that particular activity. No one who fails to see dodges like this is likely ever to become top brass. The deans themselves learn this quickly.

Except for the rule-citer, none of these administrators has serious objections to the removal of grades. Changes and deviations from the line upset some persons, but administrators do not have to grade, to suffer through the long debates over whether Joe should have a B or a C, or over the even more feckless choice between a B– or a C+. That is up to the teachers. The administrator learns to speak their various dialects. Authoritarian teachers do not speak the same language as benevolent ones and the administrator has to know what each means. His acquired adeptness at language allows him not to be greatly concerned as to whether teachers speak a language of grades or come closer to the issues at hand. He prefers the latter, however.

Description is the language of the administrator. Even teachers who use only flowery abstractions and elaborate platitudes to support grades prefer to speak their own languages, and that is also true of administrators. Although a rulebound director, when dealing with irate parents or an angry member of the faculty, can point smugly to the grade point average and the rulebook and sit tight, no one gets anywhere. The protesting person eventually departs in frustration, an unhappy outcome. Most administrators want some substantial information to back their necessary exploitations of authority.

For example, as a teacher I might claim that Joe cheated on an examination, explaining the circumstances, and add that I think he should be dismissed. The dean may know that my examinations are notoriously ridiculous and he may plan his action accordingly, an ounce of appeasement for me and a pound of justice later. If, however, I merely submit an *F* grade and keep still, the dean is forced into a corner. Living in an atmosphere of verbose academic conferences, he knows how to deal with words. The grade gives him a symbol which has a special meaning for every teacher and every situation. The *F* signifies failure but it stops there, and the dean is handcuffed.

Among specific administrative problems which concern teachers and grades, the first to appear concerns the admission of students to campuses. A university may claim, for example, that it will take all applicants who are in the top twelve percent of their high school classes. This is wonderfully simple scheme for the colleges and for teachers in high schools, especially if they are expedient graders, but it hap-

pens to ignore the welfare and education of applicants. There
are not enough expedient graders, for one thing. But all down
the years colleges have realized that admissions by means
of grades alone can be misleading. If we grant that administrators are realists who live in an academic atmosphere, this
realization is in itself an administrative declaration that
grades are not acceptable indices even of academic proficiency.

The task of securing descriptions in words for all applicants coming from high schools, let alone interpreting
them, would hardly be practical with the great stacks of
applications colleges now receive. Even so, each student
represents an investment of some ten thousand dollars. Generally thought to be more important, his education is a con-
trolling investment in major parts of his life. Each single
admission is important to the one involved. Colleges often
claim that they want only the "best material." *Best* is meaningless. The use of the word *material* exemplifies a stuffy
attitude too common in academic circles. Citizens at large,
leaving out those personally involved, want fair play.

How momentous admissions are considered to be depends on the point of view. To Joe and his family enrollment
is tremendously important. Disregarding fairness, selection is
notably less important within colleges than its faculties like
to believe. To select students by drawing straws might be
a little extreme, but not always. I have long had a nefarious
wish to try a couple of years during which applicants were
selected by quietly drawing straws, just to see how long it
would take the faculty to discover the fact. With groups
already academically screened several times, such as medical
or graduate students, the chances are good that the trick
would never be discovered. Still, we cannot afford to be
blind to the obvious: students who are adept at pleasing
teachers are likely to continue to please, more so than those

who have been frequently disapproved. One who likes the water is more likely to swim ably than one who hates it.

Colleges have depended heavily on grades to select their students. That such reports are not trusted is evident, since special tests, interviews, letters of recommendation, and general indices of various kinds have all been invoked. These are all mechanical devices aimed at critical descriptions. The question is simple: "How well will the applicant be able to use the opportunity we offer?" The answer depends on ordinary information: "Has he an active mind, is he personally adaptable to work with us, and will he work?" These simple but essential points are not reflected in grades.

The status of interviews and letters of recommendation, both of which are in theory descriptive, becomes all too clear to those who study such. Over a period of twenty years almost all of our medical students scheduled for dismissal were given cheerful praise from interviewers when they were accepted, though the only bias was that created by the applicant at the moment. Letters of recommendation usually vary in plan from "*I* regard him as worthy. Therefore you should take him." to "He performed brilliantly for us, getting one of the highest marks on his final examination. I hope you will consider him worthy." Despite the use of words, the opportunity and obligation to describe is overlooked in favor of word-grading. "I like it" is paramount.

Able admissions officers in colleges of reasonably limited size nevertheless learn to get at some descriptive data and that is what they need and want. They travel and observe environments, principals, teachers, alumni, parents, and neighbors. They get letters in which something *is* said. Not all letters of recommendation are of the "I approve" or "I am selling" variety. Interviews, based on experience and consequent caution, can bring out evidence which is factual and noteworthy.

The conclusion is inescapable. When critical decisions regarding students are mandatory, all the information which can be secured will be of help, as complete a description as is attainable. That the total will rarely be enough goes without saying, but the decision is imminent. When only a grade record is available, it is still partial evidence, but it is so misleading that the laws of chance seem virtually as useful. Reliance on the poor evidence of grades is unquestionably overdone.

When applied to high, intermediate, and early schools, the problems of grading change somewhat, though not much. Though these schools might justify grades rather better than colleges, they have accomplished more than higher education in pointing out the evils that grades produce in teaching. Thinking now of high schools as related to college, and thus including independent preparatory schools, we encounter an important but unmentioned problem in ethics. Is it ethical for colleges to demand the grades of applicants? In doing so, colleges exert pressure on schools which are not connected with them. By demanding grades, colleges and universities force preceding schools into procedures which good preparatory schools know adversely influence their teaching. The demand forces teachers into a noteworthy degree of expedient grading that it is relatively easy to excuse. The need to teach students so that they will get grades in college instead of for learning is not excusable, however.

Preparatory schools with exceptional reputations, either publicly or privately operated, are well aware that admissions officers recruit applicants as often as they screen volunteers. Colleges want students from these preparatory schools and will use scholarships, bribes, and blandishments to get them. We must credit athletic coaches with the discovery of recruiting long ago, but candidates no longer have to be stars in football.

Suppose, now, that one of these good preparatory schools, or preferably all of them, refused to grade their students because they knew the practice harmed their teaching. Surely such decisions are their own business; and good teaching is their legitimate goal. Applicants from these schools would then be unable to submit grades, since none existed. This would be a wonderful lesson to colleges. They would awaken to the fact that they needed these academically able and adequately prepared applicants, grades or not, and that they did not control schools outside their jurisdiction. Experienced admissions officers who follow their admitted students through know well the dangers of reliance on a set of cabalistic symbols which fail to meet human situations. Some of them must view with distaste the obeisance of good lower schools to the haughty demands of colleges.

Students who transfer from one school to another constitute special problems in admissions. Those who seek to transfer from one college to another vary from the occasional fellow who wants to move nearer home or where his girl friend goes to school to the numerically larger problems, such as those who transfer from junior colleges. With a large number of transferring students under a regular program the problems are much the same as those for admitting freshmen, though the farther along the student is the more helpful descriptive evidence is procurable.

With special infrequent instances of "transfer with advanced standing," grades are commonly all but ignored by those who decide, often not admissions officers. The common answer depends on the attitude of the previous college. If it would be glad to keep the applicant, the chances for safe acceptance are good, unless the deciding administrator is dubious about the other school. The incidental questions are less concerned with grades than with motives. If the motive is merely personal, the decision depends on the will and opportunity to accommodate.

On the other hand, when a student seeks to transfer to escape trouble elsewhere, the danger signal is up. The decision depends on the trouble and on the administrator. Sometimes one will accept a student who was in trouble with the previous school *because* he is doubtful about the other school. A persuasive plea by the applicant may cause an administrator to be swayed by his personal reaction unduly, also.

Older readers may recall the Finn twins, George and Charles. They were often on the front pages of newspapers because these geniuses used such outrageous means to defend their unusual acts. At one stage of their lives their obviously plausible manners secured for them a transfer between colleges. The dean who was fooled was not the only one attracted by the personable but shrewd ways of this pair, who once crossed a judge in court by defying him to tell which was which. They have not been in the news for some years, but I would bet that they were successful, and wish them luck.

Graduate schools have a relatively easy time with admissions, though deans who would own to this might be hard to find. Their applicants have had four years of experience in college, often on the same campus. A stranger could look in vain for the graduate school. It is only an administrative office which farms out all its work to others on its campus. A fetish is made of grades on entrance to graduate schools, but it is meaningless. For one reason, the school cannot accept an applicant unless some department on the campus wants him and is able to take him in to house, to teach, and usually to pay. For another reason, except for foreign students, the evidence that a student has studied is easily available. Foreign applicants can indeed be puzzling, but cer-

tainly they are not accepted on grades. They illustrate again
that desirable applicants can be recognized without grades.

One of our graduate students came from another university with a grade point average which was just a little
under par. The dean of the graduate school was a candidate
for membership in the Rulebound Administrators' Club. The
applicant, a most earnest student, was just the type the
graduate school liked, but her scholastic inclinations had led
her to take some of the toughest courses on her campus, an
act that prospective graduate students usually avoid. Her
admission depended literally on whether the graduate school
was better off with a student who had a strong preparation
in difficult courses, though the record was under the limit
established by rule, or with a student who was over the
minimum limit but had enrolled in normal or easy courses.
The dean battled with his conscience but his good judgment
won. Description, not grades, which only raised an unneces-
sary issue, provided the answers pertinent to the situation.

Those who deal with graduate students today are inclined to shrug shoulders over grades, at least after students
are accepted as candidates for advanced degrees. Usually a
B average is required. This makes only A and B grades available for such students, unless failure is intended. A few
teachers will ignore this and will give C's with little thought.
Teachers with graduate students in their mixed classes
normally recognize their presence and stretch a point, if
necessary, to use only A's and B's.

Since grading is subjective, whether we accept the idea
or not, expedience is bound to be more common than is admitted. When a graduate student or even a prospective one
who proposes to become a chemist enrolls in a class in advanced French, with majors in modern languages and in
English all around him, he can be competent and yet appear
relatively to be inept. Is the teacher to measure him with

the same yardstick, or is he to view the situation realistically? Voters for each side will appear, but I am betting on expedience, the only reasonable practice for a teacher who is denied the right to use words and is restricted to the use of vague symbols.

Teachers quite commonly protest against nongrading on the ground that transfers and graduate schools make grading obligatory to them. This brings us back to our problem in ethics. Who runs which school? Able students will be admitted and will be wanted. Grades which do not exist cannot be used. There is something pathetic about a school which uses grades daily on all students in all classes because another school chooses to ask for grades for an occasional student who transfers. And the argument is circular. Grades are in part requested because the receiving schools can so rarely secure anything else. A more normal reaction, one which would prevail if schools really considered grading procedures to be socially and educationally harmful, would be to tell any school which requested grades that only descriptive data were available. Worthy receiving schools would be pleased.

Despite current abnormal pressures by no means all of the students in undergraduate work seek entrance to a graduate school. Fortunately, by no criterion do all those who apply come from the top ten percent. The calm acceptance of grading by an entire school or college on the basis of demonstrably occasional uses is a strange form of acquiescence, even if grades were acceptable indices. Furthermore, since grades interfere with the educational process, this conformity points up a grievous but common general form of error. The rights of the many or the deserving are put aside in favor of concessions to the few, and these identifiable in other ways with no injury to them.

When the benefits to the few are unreal and justice for all is possible, wholesale grading seems really far fetched.

We like to be agreeable, we prefer peace, the customer is always right, so we give grades to schools who ask on their blank forms. When a lady takes a dress on credit, wears it to a party, and returns it, if the store lets the matter go honest customers have to meet the damages in cold cash. Appeasing such a customer is improper; the onus should fall where it is due. The experts in public relations might be surprised at how many persons would support a store which did not appease the few undeserving at the expense of the many deserving.

Standing loftily over the rest of the campus, the administrative offices labeled GRADUATE SCHOOL have a strong influence on the grading of entire undergraduate student bodies, not even limited to their own campuses. Yet the graduate school itself, seeking scholastic standards, manages to rise above grades. When it asks applicants for grades it dictates an administrative technique of profound influence on the undergraduate teaching itself, not to mention on morale and on human fates.

These upper level schools thus dictate policies to lower schools, policies which interfere with good teaching, policies which harm many who will never seek the upper levels, and policies not within the jurisdiction of the upper schools. One reason for this is that authoritative descriptive evidence is not available in the instances needed. If grading is good for teaching, so be it. If it is not, this form of control by schools or colleges is despotic, narrow, and not in the best interests either of justice or of education.

13. Subject to Dismissal

THE ADMINISTRATIVE PROBLEMS of recruiting and admitting students differ from those concerned with warnings, probations, and dismissals. For one thing, to accept half a student is impossible but, once accepted, criticism in all degrees is possible. With fewer students and ample space, acceptance of students on a trial basis was once common. This called for many later dismissals. Schools which did this paid scant attention to admissions and counted on selection by direct observations.

Today we have a reversal, with difficulties in gaining admission. Dismissals, on the other hand, have become rare. To dismiss a student now is to confess to a failure in selecting him, thus throwing the weight of guilt on the school instead of on the student. To the school acceptance of guilt is unthinkable. Besides, dismissals bring criticism from all sides. Schools are far more fond of praise, and "public relations" has come to refer to a state of almost psychopathic glorification rather than to its original meaning, amicable business is good business.

Within the operating campus, however, with its students who are officially enrolled, the maintenance of standards poses a problem. No system of admissions can be perfect, even when this goal is approached by refusing to admit that errors in judgment occur. There will be mistakes, and students are likely to deviate from anticipated paths. Pleasant or not, some provision for administrative discipline is necessary. To furnish a diploma to every freshman who entered, along with the receipt for his registration fee, would save so much worry on the part of all concerned that the procedure is tempting, but the opportunity to loaf until commencement would be unduly attractive. We might well be surprised at how few would take advantage of the situation, but weakness is inevitable. Furthermore, everyone has academic limitations.

In the jargon of the grading campus, students now and then "fall below a C average." If I so report for Joe, whom you do not know, this tells you his score but it says nothing about Joe. The routine meaning is, "Joe is not doing very well, and better be careful." "Well" and "careful" are general words of relativity.

This "C average" may be derived from a mixture of high and low grades, or each grade may be consistently low. The two situations would have quite different meanings. Investigation may show that Joe's B in Physical Education cancels his D in Physics, certainly different in their requirements, however one may view their importance. The more one pries into the situation, the more cogent become the queries about the meaning of that "below C average," until a descriptive point of view is in order. At that stage, one simply gives up and grants that "below C average" is only a sign of technical danger, justly or unjustly and for unknown reasons. The student is in jeopardy. But just what is wrong and what should or can be done about the situation?

If symbolism is imperative, and to some persons the urge to use symbols seems to be almost overwhelming, we can start by dividing the students in each course into only two sections. Without defining them, we can then ask a mathematician what symbols in man's most elegant realm of symbolism he would choose to represent two sections of a group. He perhaps will say that P and Q would be appropriate, since we are postulating only the separation of a group of integers into two parts which, together, make the whole class, C. Accepting this, let P represent the major part of the class, standing descriptively for Passed or Promoted, and signifying that members of this group no longer concern the immediate teachers, so far as Progress to the next educational step is a question. Frequently this P will include the whole class; every member moves on to the next class. The general formula is now $P + Q = C$, and in that case $Q = 0$ and $P = C$.

Since students with P go on to the attentions of their next teachers, we can now examine the Q group, a small number. Since students of the Q group are not unequivocally passed or promoted, it follows that some doubts exist about members of this group. The doubts about Joe are not at all likely to be the same as the doubts about Jane, so this symbolic approach has quite different connotations from "Not Passed," "Failed," or "below C average."

The Q group becomes the Questionable group, students about whom assorted doubts of unstated nature exist. Whereas "below C average" pretends to designate a general state of inadequate performance, calling for censure, the symbolism of Questionable says only that something needs further inquiry. The Q represents a flexible realm of the unknown, implying neither censure nor praise. With a Q, the onlooker is bound to ask "What *is* the doubt?" The Q may lead to censure, praise, or preferably only to explanation, but in all instances it leads to description. These are the students about whom we have to do something, but nothing is implied as to why or what. To use $P =$ Promoted and $Q =$ Questioned-for-reasons-unspecified is a realistic administrative procedure, far more clearly understandable than $C =$ fair and D = barely passing. It points the way to described troubles.

Teachers and administrators have to deal in some way with the Q group, students about whom some teachers have doubts. Since our point of view at the moment is administrative, let us ask the teacher who put down Q for Joe just what, specifically, his doubts are, and whether or not he has any suggestions about meeting the situation. The chances are good that the situation can be met with benefit to Joe. Despite the noncommital quality of "below C average," administrators who have to meet these same problems with only such data soon learn that students whose performances are questioned may have any of a dozen reasons for the doubts expressed. The reasons, and new ones are common, are the real statements of the problems.

Administrators have to concern themselves with students' difficulties rather than with their class standings. With grades, the student invariably supposes that a certain professor trimmed him on an unfair midterm examination. The dean may suggest vaguely that perhaps the student should not have tried out for the hockey team. The urge to put the blame on a particular incident, usually not pertinently, is strong. Excuses serve no purpose unless they reveal the real trouble, which is rarely the case. Joe may have been absent for two weeks because of illness, he may have spent too much time on extracurricular activities, he may have carried an outside job that took too much time; or perhaps he fell in love, is naturally slow, or is one of the poor readers; or possibly his father died and left him with financial worries, or he was genuinely incompatible with a teacher, for this occasionally happens. The list is by no means exhausted.

An administrator who tries to find suitable answers to determined problems may not encounter duplicate reasons for questioned students for several years. The real reasons may lie deep and are by no means always discovered. Administrators sometimes throw up their hands, granting the overwhelming nature of the difficulty at the outset without seeking causes and remedies. This can be due to the teacher's use of the mechanical means of escape, the "below C average," or the dean himself may lean on the vagueness to dodge responsibility. Deans have been known to remark sagely only that the student should have done better and then to refer him to a psychiatrist. In such instances, we shall never know how often psychiatrists see the ruse and carry on as the administrator should have done but did not, and how often they don their professional robes and seek troubles that they could find in any of us. A dismissed student once returned after a year, however, to say that he should be reinstated in medicine because the psychiatrist had told him that such would be good therapy for him. Were this advice not so discouraging and hard on the student, the switch in administrative responsibility would have been amusing.

This is not the place to review the many possible ordinary reasons for questionable performance by students and the possible ways to meet them. A dean is usually the one who has to face the problems. He acquires by trial and error such wisdom as he can attain under the vagaries of grades. The basic situation is that a teacher has questioned the work of some student and says so, causing the dean to take over and do something about it. What he does is up to the dean. If the trouble appears to be fiscal, for example, perhaps funds can be found as loans or grants. The apparent need can be genuine or it may be no more than an excuse. The dean is forced to suspect both teacher and student. I have known students to look woebegone as they seek fiscal blessings because they thought they felt that they needed a new refrigerator or a television set. One student all but demanded money so his *wife* could finish her education at another school.

Questions are most frequently raised by a single department, especially one run by a disciplinarian who is unusually skeptical about students' merits. In this case, the department should either be shaken up, which is rarely in order, or it should be satisfied. In such situations it makes little difference whether the accusation is right or wrong. The student at least cannot afford to be under a departmental cloud. And even in a case of poor judgment the department is injured when its legally proper criticisms are overridden. Arrangements to satisfy the department are in order, meanwhile protecting the student against permanent injury inflicted by a single department, unsupported in its judgment.

When several departments converge with a single point of criticism the problem takes a different form. Perhaps Joe is doing well until a slump suddenly occurs in several of his courses, with the result that Joe gets a set of Q's. In this event, surely something specific can be found as a cause of this change in performance. Whatever the reason, the chances are that the trouble can be found and met squarely.

Jane, on the other hand, perhaps started out moderately and has been getting steadily farther behind until several Q's appear. She may be slow, or possibly she was poorly prepared; and there are other possible causes. If she is too slow to keep up, soft-hearted teachers or deans will want her to take the year's work a second time, a procedure which lowers standards and can be a form of refined cruelty. Jane, otherwise a deserving person, may not be talented along academic lines. To turn her to other channels before the damage goes deeper would then be a kindness to all concerned. If all is well except for a poor preparation, however, a break which would allow her to fill in the gaps would serve well.

These are pedestrian samples of a direct and specific treatment based on the descriptive approach. When teachers pass students without fuss, all is well; if teachers raise specific questions about students, the administrator has to face realities. He has to know just what is questioned so that he can decide whether his school must dismiss, or whether it can remedy the difficulty and, if so, how. An admirable covering of the issue for the inevitable book of rules would be: "Students who do not make reasonable use of the opportunities offered may find themselves subject to disciplinary action, including dismissal." The rule will work adequately providing the school does not also wind itself up in red tape and regulations based on grades. The simple rule is enough, a manageable, specific, and reasonable starting point toward individual solutions of the problems of students whose work teachers question. The descriptive approach is flexible and realistic, making it frustrating to the rulebound tabulators. They, not the principle, need to be corrected, however.

The usual ritual for problems of doubted students in colleges is based on grades and computers. The ritual carefully avoids the human aspects, though these are common alike to administrators, teachers, and students, despite the order of authority. The general formula is to warn, put on probation, or dismiss students who fall below the so-called standard. Let us inspect this ritual in the light of nongrading.

Warning usually consists of a formal indication to the student that he better improve or things may get worse. Regardless of the difficulty a standard form is customary, perhaps a letter, a "cinch" notice from the recorder, or an oral scolding. This annoys students without providing any information. If warnings come freely or are from teachers who warn frequently, students pay scant attention. The line between warning and nagging is not a sharp one. The advisability of warning of possible disasters which students are aware of anyway can be seriously debated.

True, an occasional student may not realize that he is slipping, but the spirit of "keep up or else" is rarely appropriate, often out of place. A letter of warning was sent once to one of our students. His work during the following term was entirely satisfactory and he was returned to a normal status. This good recovery caused the uninitiated to gloat vocally; they were sure that the warning had led to the improved performance. In this case, however, the student dropped in to ask the meaning of the letter he had received, congratulating him and saying that he had been removed from the warning status. He had been off working in the deep woods during the preceding summer and had never received his warning. So much for its effect!

The routine procedure is supposed to be more significant when a student is put on *probation*. Under the computer, a student falls "below a C average." He then gets word from the dean telling him that he is on probation. The official letter may be personally addressed and signed but all letters sent out will be alike. When Joe gets his letter he knows that his work has disturbed his teachers in some unknown manner. He inquires among his associates. If he discovers that a number in his class also were put on probation, he will compare his tactics with those of other students, shine apples for his teachers, and otherwise forget the matter.

A careful administrator will use probation with marked care. The effect on conscientious students who are already doing their best can be traumatic for them and poor for their studies. A promiscuous use of probation, presumed to keep students on their toes, will also more often discourage or antagonize than help. The word *probation* has the same origin as *proof* and the use should be confined to those who, for known justifiable reasons, may legitimately be asked to prove their worth. To determine the probationary status by pouring grades into a computer and pressing a button puts in the same boat the slow but conscientious student, the smart hell-raiser, the fellow who puts "campus activities" first, and the student who goes to too many movies and parties. This is a heinous offense against good teaching.

Another such noteworthy offense occurs when probation fails to mean what it says. In effect, it says that "you may be subject to dismissal next term unless your work is in every way satisfactory." Probation, used exceptionally, can be entirely proper when it serves to apply severe censure to students who presumably could do much better work. They are thus put on trial and given the choice between going to work and going home. This is a major justification for several possible circumstances which may warrant probations, so let us look at it more carefully.

At the end of the probationary term for Joe the sage advisors inspect his work, seeking to judge whether or not it has improved and is satisfactory, as was stipulated in the probationary status. Joe is still in the Q category, not entirely satisfactory, so he should be ready for dismissal.

Teachers and administrators, usually ready enough to put students on probation, dislike to take the next promised step. It has cost them few pangs and no hazards to put Joe on probation, to give him the frown of displeasure, but to dismiss him is distasteful and causes repercussions. The result is that probation becomes a temporizing move which does not consider Joe's status as much as it puts those who sit in judgment in a position to act, if they should choose, at some vague future date. When the date arrives, however, and Joe is still in the Q group, the authorities get squeamish. They try to frown ever more sternly, promise to act *next* time, and continue probation. Probation then becomes no more than a series of meaningless threats.

This undermines the whole purpose. Probation becomes something for students to laugh at and to make teachers feel unsupported and insecure. When probation is not definitely pertinent it should never be used. More often than not it is not necessary; the *reasons* for Q are many, and judgment requires specific observations, not grade point averages.

Coming to the hot waters of *dismissal*, emotions have to be held in check. Dismissal is surgery and it hurts, but it can be a kindness. A decision rather than a move for moral effect, dismissal also should be used only when it is fitting, albeit for the good of the student, his fellow students, the teachers, or the school. Dismissal for the peace of mind of the administration and teachers is dubious. With fields such as engineering, medicine, law, or dentistry, for the protection of citizens at large a student's integrity as well as his work is at stake. Able students who lack integrity probably do not belong in any professional group, since we are all helpless when we put our trust in the hands of specialists, but some professions can be less harmful than others.

The precaution that dismissal should be meaningful at first glance seems needless. One college made dismissal practically equivalent to probation. It gravely dismissed students with little compunction whenever the teachers raised any marked fuss. Any sensitive teacher, however, might cause cases to be reopened and usually the student was allowed to return. That such equivocation was a form of expedient paternalism which disrupted the morale of both teachers and students goes without saying. Dismissal requires all possible care; but, when the decision is made, it has to be clear cut and final, with the sympathetic ones and those who disagree standing with the majority.

With dismissals the headaches are many. The only basic remedy is to try to do the right thing, come what may. Teachers are human and have soft spots. One who votes for dismissal at a meeting may encounter the victim within the hour and, feeling a little guilty, tell the student how well he did on his final examination. Teachers have been known to weaken and to call up a dean at night to say that, though they voted for dismissal with the evidence before them, they now think the decision really was too drastic.

Classes or fraternities may send their officers to headquarters with wild tales, based wholly on rumors. They usually arrive with obvious chips on their shoulders, but they are also usually ready to listen to the facts and scotch the rumors, if such they prove to be. Parents may send wires to the president of the university or to their legislators, and the president may telephone to the school with fire in his voice.

But when the investigation behind dismissal is careful and there is descriptive evidence to back the dismissal, with no signs of later weakness, the tones quickly change. The president, for example, knows that vacillation after careful judgments makes matters worse. Some decisions have to stand. A student once told his dean that dismissal relieved his mind and was a blessing. To save face, however, this student told quite a different story to his classmates. The classmates were wrathy. Subsequent events proved that each of the dismissed student's stories contained some truth. He was grateful, but also resentful and unsuited to the work.

Dismissal is awkward and discouraging for the victims, but so are many parts of life. The one move that cannot be made gracefully is to equivocate. A dean who listens to members of his faculty when they object to a legitimately judged dismissal and, based on pleas or other than substantial evidence of factual error, begins to wobble, is confessing that his own investigation has been improper. All investigations have weak spots, but at this stage shiftiness undermines the morale of everybody concerned.

One may safely postulate in advance that every dismissed student will have friends, relatives, and sympathetic listeners. This is fortunate, for dismissals are not often to be interpreted as censure. Dismissal indicates only a lack of performance in a given restrictive field, not in all fields. The reasons for the act may be quite acceptable, with no blame attached. Occasionally, for example, the weak performance of a medical student is inadvertently or otherwise deliberate, due to parental pressure which forced the student into a field for which he had neither taste nor talent.

Whether dismissal should always be preceded by probation or some form of warning is a moot question over which debates can be violent. Nearly everyone would agree that flagrant situations might call for a peremptory dismissal, but these are rare. Not all agree, however, that dismissal for scholastic deficiencies without a previous warning can be permissible. The general vague feeling of objectors seems to be that such a dismissal is like shooting a man in the back.

On the theory that rules should be few and flexible, the *requirement* of a previous warning seems unfortunate. Beyond question, it is a decent thing to do for a dubious student who has to choose between working reasonably hard and gambling that he can get by with indifferent effort. On the other hand, some situations cannot be eased, and these are not always wisely anticipated. There is no easy way to tell a person that the other fellow got the promotion or that a friend is dead. To build up concern over dismissal for longer than a few moments can be refined cruelty.

There are situations in which a student should be dismissed at the end of a term without previous warning. A conscientious, nervous, and slow student, for instance, has the anticipation of failure hanging over him or her constantly, without warnings. An official warning only increases the strain and makes learning more difficult, providing an added handicap to one who already has too many. To handicap smart students who fail to use their talents because they see no need for the effort is another matter altogether. The ballplayer who plays five games without getting a hit is dismayed. He knows that he may be sent back to the minor

leagues or at least be benched for a while. It is not necessary
to nag at him with warnings; to do so may spoil his chances
of success. If the manager has to send him back, no pre-
liminary warning is formally necessary or wise.

Notification of possible dismissal through warnings is
complicated by the significant percentage of the Q students
who pay little attention to formal warnings. When such students are dismissed later, they will claim vigorously that they
had not been warned, even though a dozen forms of warning can be proved and even though the lack of warning
would prove nothing about ability, promise, or effort. Such
students make so much noise that deans, feeling guilty, may
swear publicly never to dismiss a student without previous
warning, in writing, an outlook which is likely to lead to a
plethora of warnings as a form of insurance. The promise
sounds reassuring to students until troubles occur. Educationally, the whole matter of warning should be flexible.
Based on specific information instead of on grade points, this
specific treatment and flexibility is a certainty.

A new attitude toward dismissal, as generous as the
situation allows, is in order. When the evidence indicates
that nothing but trouble can arise along the academic path
being followed, the chances are that the student has potential ability in a number of other ways. The school is not
censuring. It would like to help him in any promising work
except the troublesome one, for which it is responsible.
Whether dismissal or gold medals are in order, academic
proficiency is the narrowly implied limit. If we grade, that
means only the degree of expertness in getting grades.

An inspection of these administrative problems can leave
no doubt but that pooled decisions, not made by teachers
or their departments, will be more specific, more judicious,
and more often fair when teachers turn in their observations
on Q students, rather than final judgments expressed in one

of six vague symbols. Why handicap administrators who, based on observations made by teachers, have to make decisions critical for students?

14. Beyond the Classroom

ONCE THE PRINCIPLE OF NONGRADING is thoroughly in mind, it will reappear in various guises outside the classroom, contrasted with the principles of grading. Grading is a habit, unduly subjective and casual in its emphasis on personal preferences. This same stress on preference distracts from the extension of less subjective powers of observation, for description demands observation and specificity.

The distinctions between sorting, evaluation, and grading need to be kept clearly defined. Sorting is a process occurring hourly in our lives for the sake of order and convenience. Microbiologists spend many hours in identifying or sorting microorganisms, which they neither evaluate nor grade. Clothing stores sort garments by sizes, else the clerks and customers would find chaos. One of the neatest bits of sorting occurs with a notably impersonal recognition of man's individualism. Put "K. Jones, Norwell, MA 02061" on a postal card and, should there be such a person, the card would go promptly not only to the right house but to the right person in the house, a single one of 3,000,000,000 persons in the world to whom it might have gone.

Evaluation, on the other hand, implies quantification and analysis. The quantification arises because a scale of values is intrinsic in the thought of setting a value upon something, and quantification demands a scale and a pointer. The *relative* position on the scale is implied. A scale of values also implies that all concerned participate in a stipulated scheme of values. If the system is fiscal, we agree to the law of supply and demand, or some system of worth to those concerned. Ultimately evaluation comes back to preference, or what an item is worth to us. Gold is valueless to a person dying of thirst in a desert. The analysis comes about because relative positions can be set only if we inspect things to which an item is relative, noting enough of the several features to place its position on our scale of values.

Evaluation is thus intensely personal. What is given a high value by you, perhaps a piece of Limoges china, may be valueless to me. Evaluation in a broad sense is a process of sorting, but the basis of sorting, convenience, is only incidental. What it is worth to me is the crucial issue.

Offhand, grading appears to be similar to evaluation, or to be a special form of it, but the resemblance is misleading. The grading process does combine the orderliness of sorting, for a particular bit of convenience, with the setting of relative values of preference. It transcends convenience, however, and pretends to values which are not there. Intrinsic worth is implied, and in the story of a complex person, a student, there is no such thing. That this so-called intrinsic worth can be estimated accurately, the quantification of evaluation, is likewise a myth. It cannot be accurately estimated both because of personal involvement and because it is not there. That the personal preference or estimate of worth is valid in personal evaluation can be supported; but in grading the process becomes little more than a capricious set of ambiguities.

The backgrounds of these concepts are distinctive, no matter how easy it is to quibble over similarities. We might *grade* apples according to size, thus *sorting* them for the convenience of setting fancy *values* on the larger ones. Even in this simple example the three distinctive features stand out. Students are not apples; and apples do not have complicated futures.

Description, the fourth choice, calls for a flat reporting of observations, without bias. The lack of bias is, of course, hypothetical. The poet, artist, and photographer describe the same scene quite differently. We cannot avoid reading ourselves into description, sorting, evaluating, or grading. We can, however, come closer to specificity through description; and in so doing we can frankly reveal the biased fraction of ourselves, so that the bias may be included as part of the story, rather than blindly or blandly denied.

The habit of grading permeates our lives. How much of this is due to habits formed during schooling and how much to the dominance that personal choice attains with each of us is anyone's guess.

Certainly the habit acquired from schools is responsible for the testing services ruled by psychologists, whereby an adult, ten years out of college with a family to support, finds himself graded on a battery of questions made out by persons unfamiliar both with the work he proposes to do and with the conditions of the company, a grading system which is called impersonal chiefly because it allows executives to escape their responsibilities for judgment in hiring and promoting their staffs. Fortunately, many companies refuse to do this, but schools, anxious for their students to get ahead, meanwhile try to prepare students to meet such social notions, thereby setting up a circular action.

Had they the courage of their convictions, colleges would object to such moves; but they would have to begin by eliminating grading within their own walls.

The tendency to exclaim at length about one's likes and dislikes of almost anything to some persons is irresistible. In daily living this is harmless and can add zest to life. Teachers of English, however, and editors, have troubles with this habit, akin to grading. They protest against mere exclamation, because they know that readers care little about someone's likes and dislikes but want to know *what* there is to enjoy, quarrel with, or use. When description is used, the reader can do his own deciding about approval, indifference, or disapproval. In some degree we are all guilty. Billions of words have been uttered or written about Exposition 67 in Montreal. How many of them, would you guess, told nothing about it but conveyed simply a personal grading, an impression?

Among intimates and up to a point, this grading or expression of choice may be justified. The emotional reaction of a child, parent, or close friend may be more interesting or pertinent for the listener than their descriptive bases for the reaction, yet even in this situation the reason for the intimate's preference is more informative and pertinent than the preference itself. Someone who has seen a certain movie speaks about it to a friend who has not. The speaker gives his reactions but says nothing about the movie or the basis for his reactions. A close friend conceivably may not want to hear about the movie; he may prefer to hear about the reaction.

Even in this extreme, however, lurking in the background is the elf who remarks that it is wiser to say something specific than to express preferences. "I was enraptured" means less than "I thought the color was beautiful;" "I thought it was awful" is not on a par with "That gruesome stuff could appeal only to sadists." Note that *beautiful, gruesome,* and *sadists* are all emotional words. One who is a nongrader at heart might say "The color was brilliant" or "There was a lot of gore in the picture." Teachers and students need a focus, and so do ideas and words. The teacher who gives an A has said no more than "I like it." To stifle emotions would be absurd, but to restrict the graded variety of conversation and writing would vastly improve both. Grading is more than a classroom routine; it is a broad bad habit.

Consider also the semantic angle of grading. We acquire semantic concepts by putting personal expansions on words until their meanings become warped. Consider such words as *Nazi, Communism, Republican, Democrat, welfare, extremism, war, religion, aristocrat, slave, rights,* and so on. Even such words as *linguistics,* originally solid words used in differentiating ideas, have become emotional terms. Connotations become barnacles on words, slowing them down and all but destroying their usefulness, equally true whether the words arouse bitter antagonism or sturdy defense. The semantic deviations in *A = excellent* allow persons to become scornful, smug, happy, satisfied, or envious, all because of expanded personal connotations.

The habit of grading causes us to take small parts of the meanings of words and to exaggerate them into generalities which match our approvals or disapprovals. This causes us to condemn or applaud persons or groups, and sometimes inanimate items, for qualities which they do not have. It is quite customary to blame the "other" person for virtually anything that goes wrong. It is wiser, safer, calmer, and more meaningful to describe than to grade. Suppose that I say "Demoblicans are fools." You learn only that I do not like them. Fools are foolish persons, so in a sense I have described them as I saw them, but the generalization is really only a relative word, like *good* or *bad.* The comment becomes no more than a personal blanket judgment. I have put a pointer on the scale of my own opinions, implying that the value of my personal degree of approval is absolute and is sufficient.

I have issued a fiat but I have said nothing. I gave the Demoblicans an *F*.

Ultimately the habit of grading is seen as a habit of weighing everything in relative terms of preference rather than observing. Personal reactions of importance only to the speaker formulate a scale of ranking which is imposed on others. Everything, instead of being different from something else, becomes vaguely better or worse. Instead of liking Golden Delicious apples because they are slightly sweet, mild, and do not discolor quickly, and last through the winter, you may prefer Gravensteins. You prefer the flavor, the tartness, or perhaps without realizing it you like them because the season is short. To say that the Gravenstein is *better* than the Golden Delicious, or vice versa, is meaningless.

If, as occurs when we grade students, the lives of growers of apples are vitally affected by such grading without specific information, the practice of relative approval and disapproval, when of dubious merit, becomes seriously destructive, even though we seem to be harmlessly grading apples. If we are talking together about apples, the conversation is then futile. The Golden Delicious is not a better or worse apple; it has certain qualities. When we choose for a special purpose we are then coming to a decision by analysis of specific description.

Grading is notably introspective, whatever the claimants for alleged objectivity may say. But under descriptive practice the speaker, writer, or thinker becomes the spectator, since he has no immediate responsibilities for judgment, even though he may be setting the stage for later judgment, if required. He expresses what he sees that is pertinent to the situation. He becomes disinterested in preference, judgment, or the sorting of described qualities as faults or virtues, each of which moves will have different answers among different persons. He sees what he sees. The constant classification of observations as virtues or faults is usually unwise and is seldom necessary. He declines to accept the rules of litmus paper, forever turning blue or pink. He tries to be carefully observant. For these reasons he leans toward fairness, listening, and calmness, and away from attitudes which cause the faces of chronic graders to turn from pink to red, purple, or white, depending on whether or not events go their personal ways.

Employers are interested primarily in talent, the will to work, and integrity, relative to the work at hand. Perhaps eventually parents will realize that they are interested in character, the proper use of talents, and in the preparation for harmonious niches for their children's lives; and they are not interested in having their children merely beat the neighbor's children on a scale of who most pleased teachers, persons who, in all likelihood, parents would prefer that their children not imitate too closely. Possibly one of the best tributes to Phi Beta Kappa might be to note the number of members who do not wear their pins, who do not regard themselves as exceptionally deserving, and who do not need the prop of membership to sustain their morale.

Imperfect though it will always be, the descriptive approach to teaching students will eventually gain recognition. The weaknesses of description lie in those who use it. The weaknesses in grades lie in the disturbing principles of the system itself.

Description will at least afford some help to students, deans, employers, and parents. Description requires its users to stand back of their comments and, if need be, alter them. Description, carried beyond the classroom, becomes a calmer and more considerate outlook than that of grading everything by preference. But above all description, especially if used as occasionally as possible and with a light touch, depending

on pertinent qualities which come to the surface despite all
efforts to forget such matters, allows teachers to teach. They
are then allowed to work with their students, to look them
in the eye, to forget the class as such and to think only of
individuals, to seek development of what lies within each
student without concern over estimates of how much, to
cease to classify everything as a virtue or fault, to wrap themselves up in their subjects and their students instead of in
judgments of value, to drill less toward points they can grade
and to work harder on understanding, to worry less about
whether Joe and Jane reach the same level or some chosen
level in their work and comprehension, and to think and
write not in a few symbols for words but with the vast range
of the words themselves.

In debates about grades recurrent bugaboos arise need-
lessly. One that usually appears first is that rules or rulers of
"my" school or, worse, rules of another school, demand
grades. A second serious recurrent argument is that no satisfactory substitute for grading exists.

To the first of these objections, two answers are necessary. First, battering one's head against a wall accomplishes
nothing but injury. If the teacher is stuck under rules and
rulers, so be it. *But,* it is possible to disband grades in mind
and, in a surprising degree, in fact. Grades are not necessary
on every move, and the most can be made of nongraded
opportunities. Grades may not be required except at the end
of a course, thus allowing a whole term of teaching. At the
close of the term, descriptions are easily convertible, if necessary. Perhaps even at the end of a term only one grade can
be used, or perhaps two grades, one fairly well up and one
definitely down. To my mind ethically, teachers who have
no alternatives should not hesitate to use grades as their
votes for what they think should happen to the student. A

surprising amount of personal shift to nongrading is possible, even under an enforced grading system.

As for the objection that there is no substitute, one is recorded herein, not so much as a detailed recipe for action as a principle. It has been tried on medical, dental, dental hygiene, pharmacy, nursing, undergraduate, and graduate students, and closely followed through internships, dismissals, recommendations, scholarships, honors, and careers, for over thirty years.

The alternative to grades is description, a minimal amount of tacit recognition of pertinently floating qualities and characteristics. Not only will dedicated teachers bless this opportunity, but students will, too, while they are benefiting by better teaching. And administrators, employers, and others will heave a sigh and say "at long last"—except those to whom rites, rules, and rituals are more important than the things with which these three R's deal. Do not forget the dean who objected vigorously to a move unanimously approved. "But there is no place on the card for it," he said.

Teaching is a privilege, as well as an obligation, of those who are hired to teach. Grading is a restriction on teaching. The floating description, concise and really descriptive, is as far as a teacher need go in any record. Even that is usually too much, because so little of it is ever needed.

15. Some Applications

THE PRECEDING PAGES discuss principles of thought and action which constitute a basis for the condemnation of grades and for a lightened attitude toward the whole topic. Among the objectives of grades, however, are services as aids in making certain necessary decisions. Elimination of these decisions is not reasonably possible. Specific description, aimed at these objectives and no more, will fill the requirements more clearly, meanwhile getting rid of many of the difficulties to which the relative ranking of students gives rise.

Those involved in grading, through their interest or because of necessity, range in attitude from those who, with little personal concern, accept the status quo to those who are fully aware of the damage done in our schools due to the stress on grades. Few, even of those most aware of the unfortunate effects on teaching, however, have experience with any genuine nongrading procedures.

The principles established are substantially two. First, the grading system, including most suggested substitutes because they also use symbols or words which rank students relative to one another, can be replaced only by attaining a clean break, a genuine nongrading concept. Second, it is possible during most days with classes to ignore relative appraisal altogether and, when called upon to do so, to replace it with pertinent description based on salient or outstanding features.

It may now be helpful to present a brief formulary for the use of the unfamiliar descriptive method, on the supposition that examples and suggestions, though poor substitutes for experience, may be helpful guides. The results of many years of trial do not necessarily provide the best solutions to the applications of the principles involved. The principles stand staunchly on their own supports, but the techniques in using them are always open to improvements.

But descriptions can be endless:

To approach a student with a deliberate goal of getting data and describing his characteristics would be to return to grading, and worse. Two rules have to be held in mind.

First, grading symbols, along with such relative words as *good* or *excellent,* have to be put in the background and kept there, by deliberate effort. The habit dies with difficulty. This gives teaching its proper place, with a focus on the student and on the subject, and appraisal is put aside. True, the irritating student, the weak student, the pathetic student, or the smart student may sometimes appear early in a course. Even so, each is an individual, to be treated as a person.

Second, just as the irritating student was marked on the first day, as the course continues *dominant* features of a number of students will unwittingly appear. By ignoring all appraisal while the tasks at hand prevail, these floating features will stand out for each one in most members of a class, if contacts are even reasonably close. Description is not a goal; it is an acceptance of the inevitable, a recognition of characteristics which stand out willy-nilly. These, and primarily only these, are individual and pertinent. Restricting descriptions to dominant features reduces the descriptive method, which at first looks overwhelming, to a practical magnitude.

But teachers have to distinguish between good and bad work:

This is a common but misleading idea. It happens to be incorrect. It is not up to a teacher to distinguish between what he calls faults and what he calls virtues. It is up to a teacher to guide each individual student, who can grow necessarily only from within, to advance beyond the point at which he started in his knowledge and more particularly in his understanding of the subject. If he starts low and moves ahead, fine; when he starts high and goes no higher, something is missing.

The judgment of virtues and faults is up to those who have to make decisions which affect the student's status. These essential decisions differ widely in nature. A virtue here may be a fault there, automatically invalidating the best teacher's general estimate When a teacher faces some- one who makes decisions, but not otherwise, the person who has been nearest to the student, the teacher, is responsible for specific pertinent information. Those who decide are not asking the teacher to judge for them; they are asking for information which will help them to decide. In dealing with an honor society, for example, one set of characteristics is significant; with a potential employer, another set comes under consideration.

Why not catalogue pertinent features?

Prepared forms or lists destroy the whole principle. No two students are alike. The basic idea in flotation is to let such distinctive and definitive features as may be noted to rise to the surface of their own accord. Only one or two of any list of qualities would fit, and important occasional ones would be missing. Students are individuals and so are teachers and their subjects of study. To waste time and thought on features which do not stand out is more than wasteful. The inevitable result of the prepared formula for description is not only exhaustive emphasis on insignificant points but also a masking of the salient points.

Are not descriptions unduly biased?

Descriptions and grades, both subjective, are necessarily biased. One of the demonstrated values of description, however, is that it pulls away from biases and puts labels on those that remain.

It is imperative that teachers assume full responsibility for their own deeds. Just as they are known when they face a student personally, they should initial or sign the written criticisms and advice which appear on papers and in records. Everyone concerned knows who is speaking; the same should be true with words on paper.

To whom do these descriptions go?

Teachers are polarized, one pole pointed toward the student and the other toward legitimately interested outsiders. Since the main function of a teacher is to teach, during a course every bit of description, duly signed, goes to the student to help him while teaching continues. Properly, this will include a vast amount of personal aid that never appears in the record book. The record book needs only a summary, but it too goes to the student so long as the course is under way. Descriptive commentary then should be designed to help in some way. It should say something; words are precious, not to be wasted.

At the teacher's other pole records have to be matched to contingencies which may arise, normally promotions, probations, dismissals, transfers, honors, employment, and graduation. Were it not for these necessary activities, the whole matter could well be forgotten. These are major functions which grades try so poorly to meet.

There are several categories of potential records. Some of the commentary goes to students. Some teachers keep personal notes as ancillary records, retained by them. Comments are needed for the department's records, some word has to be sent to the recorder, and selected comments are later demanded of teachers and departments by legitimate inquiry. Some records cease to be; they go in the wastebasket, and good riddance.

We have debated this at home, but . . .:

Yes, grades are controversial, which accounts for that "but." Grades are too often fruitlessly debated. To set them against Passed/Failed, Passed/Not Passed, the use of relative words, or redefinitions of the symbols is only uselessly to compare members of the same species. To accomplish any progress grades have to be set against something which is usable and totally different in concept. Grading, false measures of purported values, ranking, and relativity can be contrasted with pertinent description and an elimination of the personal concern over values as such. The characteristic, not its value, is significant. It becomes a value only when appropriately used. Slowness is not a sin; it characterizes. Brilliance is a virtue only when it is properly applied in the right place; it can mark a fault.

Regardless of the current system used in his or her school, this altered outlook, with practice, can be attained by a willing individual teacher and to some extent it can be used.

Show us an example of a departmental record:

Here is a record based on a course in microbiology. It included laboratory work and, put in its simplest form, it referred to midterms and a final examination.

JOE Q. DOAKES

1ST MIDTERM: *You show a lot of ingenuity. It would be better if it were backed by more information* (MLP). *Better get after it and learn some facts* (NJI). [These records are summaries made by readers of the papers. They are copied into the records from the tops of the examination papers before returning them to the students.]

2ND MIDTERM: *You seem to be getting the idea in the laboratory but it does not show on the paper here* (MLP). *You are coming along well, but there is more. Keep it up* (BHU).

FINAL: *He uses what information he has in haphazard fashion, but O. K.* (MLP). *Not well informed on what I read, but adequate* (NJI). *He tries hard but seems to go off on a tangent to the question* (BHU). [These commentaries are only for the record. Time for teaching has passed, and papers are not returned.]

TERMINAL COMMENTS: *He will graduate, but I worry about a slap-dash quality* (MLP). *Smart enough, but his care and accuracy leave something to be desired* (NJI). *I think he tried hard, but the results did not always come off* (BHU).

Spread over a period of sixteen weeks, these remarks are not unduly burdensome. The name of the observer is always included. Note that the midterm examinations are given during the teaching term, and all reports go back to the student. Final examinations were not returned, however, and the terminal comments are also only for the department.

Joe emerges as a partially defined person. He is perhaps unlikely to become a great man, but he by no means is a prospective failure. Some estimates can be made not only from the descriptive remarks but from those that are not there. You might employ him summers in a filling station, but hesitate to have him take care of your weather gauges during your vacation.

How do these records concern your makers of decisions?

The easiest answer is the one for the *recorder*. His office needs to know only how many units of work have been passed for the degree. To be sure, recorders are always pestered for transcripts of records. If the school decides in favor of good teaching, with no grades, however, that is it. The recorder shows 180 units of completed work in the listed courses that were taken and passed. For more information, askers have to seek other sources, closer to classrooms and observers.

The *honor society* may want nominations. The record shows:

> *He'll probably get the gold-headed cane but he is more politic than comprehending* (VCY). *A brilliant fellow, work very impressive* (CFT). *He works no harder than he needs to but is careful to make a good impression* (SDR).

Suppose that you are in the honor society, choosing. Do you want him? True, getting an answer by a computer would be easier, but behind the figures in the computer are these same thoughts, lost in the maelstrom of grades.

A departmental record is cited above, but more specifically a letter would be written in answer to an inquiry. It might read:

> *Mr. Harry Doakes appeared to us to have a good mind and he will undoubtedly impress many persons. Just how well he is using his mind, however, has aroused*

some questions in the department. If your selections are based on quick minds and probable success, our estimate is that you would not go amiss in taking Mr. Doakes.

The *scholarship* committee perhaps wants a statement about Henry Doakes. The book says:

Worked hard but handicapped by a night job (RLK). *Seems to understand well what he gets but feel that he could do much better* (JFR). *A solid citizen, making use of his opportunities* (RBH).

To this inquiry, the scholarship committee might be informed:

Mr. Henry Doakes seemed to our staff to show considerable promise. One member mentioned that night employment at a filling station was probably a handicap. Since future promise is a critical feature in decisions about financial aid projected into future work, we are glad to have an opportunity to support this application.

Realize that the writer of the letter can amplify the record by oral discussion with anyone who recalls Henry. Note also that Henry may be the only one in a class of eighty about whom such inquiry is made. The answer is in focus.

The *dean* may be worried about probation. Philip Doakes' record reads:

Smart fellow but does a minimum amout of work (JPM). *Seems to be avidly interested in everything except our subject* (TAB). *Don't doubt his ability but doubt his graduation. Lazy* (WIL).

The dean is then informed as follows:

Philip Doakes appears to have ability but he has given us every evidence of failing to use it to take advantage of his opportunities. We would suggest that the probationary status might stir him to action.

A real problem of dismissal arises with Mitchell Doakes, so we look over his record:

> *Worked all the angles to avoid working* (BAR). *Did little work and seems to lack all sense of honest purpose* (CJL). *Came through with nothing which showed understanding. Do not trust him* (HIP).

With this record, even an outsider unacquainted with the student, unable to make inquiries of members of the staff, and unfamiliar with the commentators might be ready to say:

> *Mr. Mitchell Doaks was doubted in this department as to integrity of act and purpose, and his understanding of the subject was notably inadequate. We would have to favor dismissal on grounds of marked failure to utilize the opportunities offered to reasonable advantage.*

Letters of *recommendation* are sought for varieties of purposes, ranging from transfer to employment. Consider the record of James Doakes:

> *Slow but painstaking. Would trust him anywhere* (KRC). *One of the most reliable men in the class* (FLM). *Understanding comes hard but he retains what he gets and uses it wisely* (HEB).

No set of symbols can help in this situation, but the verbal record does:

> *James Doakes has applied to you for employment. We had him with us in microbiology in a course of sixteen weeks, during which five persons observed his work and his performance in the laboratory. Although we knew him four years ago, we have no present hesitation in recommending him on grounds of reliability, dedication to his work, and promise of continued improvement which he demonstrated with us. He was not a particu-*

*larly quick student but he made haste slowly and surely,
and we liked his willingness and his integrity.*

These illustrations do far more than explain in words
what is behind grades, for they are specific and uncritical,
and they are fitted to the occasions of legitimate demand in
the several situations. The person who makes a request
acquires some definite and pertinent observation which he
can weigh with other information. Specific and focused information is useful; a poll of opinions is mechanical and
hides the bases for them.

Not infrequently, with a letter of recommendation it is
possible effectively to cite verbal comments in quotation
marks. For instance:

*Mr. James Doakes impressed one of our experienced
laboratory observers as follows: "Slow but painstaking.
Would trust him anywhere," and other comments are
consistent with this. Taken verbatim from our records,
this citation carries the initials of a member of the staff
who had one of the best records of any in our group in
making observations later substantiated by other
evidence. . . .*

Can all teachers learn to describe succinctly?

Some do not do well, but experience suggests that the
grades given by such teachers are even worse. With words,
furthermore, deficiencies usually show. But even one word—
lazy, indifferent, quick, rattles, or pugnacious, for example—
is more informative than 76, 75, 87, 80, 83. At the other extreme, the burden of effort will usually curtail any excess
of description, except on rare occasions when amplified explanation is in order.

It is true that some observers show exceptional judgment
and others show little, just as it is true that some are harsh

critics and others are unduly generous. This is largely overcome by a record which shows who made each comment.
The harsh critic and the generous observer both use specific
words for each student, and those can be interpreted in the
light of the commentator. The method asks for specific
description, be it mild or rough. This problem is only the
difference among "What the Devil do you think you are
doing?", "Are you sure that you are getting that right?", and
"Don't you think this way would be better?" All these inquiries can pertain to the same specific act.

Since these unavoidable vagaries also exist under grades,
it seems clear that description pins down the facts better
than do grades which mask the vagaries.

Are there axioms or formulae for all this?

Indeed there are. Stop me when you have had enough.

1. $R = T \times E$ (the Results = the Talent times the
   Effort expended).
2. $C = P + Q$ (the total number in a given Class = the
   students Promoted plus those for any reason
   Questioned).
3. Description is subjective. Grades are more so.
4. To confine teachers to a set of symbols is to curb
   free speech.
5. Grading is ingrained from years of practice. To remove the habit from mind takes practice, too.
6. Teachers are employed to enjoin the subjects taught
   with their students. They are not hired to appraise
   their neighbors' sons and daughters.
7. Those who lack ability to describe also lack ability
   to grade. Those who do not have enough information
   to describe have not enough to grade, either.
8. Every student has to find his niche.

9. The test is whether words state an opinion (grading) or report an observation (description).

10. The starting point for description is a plain sheet of paper, not a form which leads and homogenizes description. When the paper remains blank, that is in itself a description.

11. Compatibility with teachers is not proof of merit; incompatibility is not proof of fault or genius. When either is unanimous, it is coincidence or a sign of trouble.

12. Discipline is a problem in schools, but not an academic one.

13. Students do not have to do what they are asked to do for their courses; schools do not have to work with students who reject the opportunities offered to them.

14. Offering work which is over the head of the fastest student will not harm the slowest student so long as nongrading prevails and all students progress.

15. To tell a student he is wrong will cause him to guess until he is "right;" to tell him *what* is wrong and why will cause him to concentrate on corrective moves.

This could continue, but that is enough.

To be effective the nongrading point of view has to exist in outlook as well as in act. The major reason that the frame of mind takes time and practice to acquire is because grading has become so deeply entrenched. That is why nongrading is really the elimination of a bad habit rather than the establishment of a good one. This creates a vacuum which can be filled by an expedient description born of necessary decisions. Imperfect though the observations in words may be, their use is a normal procedure, one which brings available evidence to bear on essential decisions, and otherwise allows teachers to ignore the whole matter and to go back to teaching.

Let those who doubt look over their records of two years ago and note how few of them have served any real purpose. Think of the energy wasted. Note how the real difficulties of students cancel each other under symbols which pool everything, thereby dodging and hiding the difficulties altogether.

The curtailed descriptive approach is possible, it fits the individual roles of teaching, and it meets all contingencies, not perfectly but reasonably and honestly.